No Experience Necessary

No Experience Necessary

Kelly A. Fryer

Augsburg Fortress
MINNEAPOLIS

NO EXPERIENCE NECESSARY
Revised and Expanded

Unless otherwise noted, Scripture quotations are from New Revised Standard Version Bible, copyright © 1989 Division of Christian Education of the National Council of the Churches of Christ in the United States of America. Used by permission.

Scripture quotations marked New Living Translation are from the Holy Bible, New Living Translation, copyright © 1996. Used by permission of Tyndale House Publishers, Inc., Wheaton, Illinois 60189. All rights reserved.

Content editors: Gloria E. Bengtson and Laurie J. Hanson

Production editor: James Satter

Series logo, cover, and interior design: Marti Naughton

ISBN 0-8066-4808-2

The paper used in this publication meets the minimum requirements of American National Standard for Information Sciences—Permanence of Paper for Printed Library Materials, ANSI Z329.48-1984.

Manufactured in U.S.A.

09 08 07   2 3 4 5 6 7 8 9 10

*In honor of Aunt Minnie and
Aunts Hazel, Gen, and Ruth—
each of whom probably never knew
exactly how important they were.
Thank you.*

Contents

PREFACE

During the summer of 1998, I spent two weeks writing the first very rough draft of *No Experience Necessary: On-the-Job Training for a Life of Faith*. I never imagined it would become a book or be published. I certainly never expected to become a "writer."

I wrote that manuscript for Lori.

Lori had come to the congregation I was serving as pastor a couple of years before. She had been raised in a church-going family but, for a lot of reasons, hadn't had a relationship with the church for a really long time. Her life had taken more than a few sharp turns.

When Lori walked into our worship service for the first time, it was because she had been invited by some friends who thought we might have something she needed. We did. But she was scared. She was afraid of not fitting in and being judged.

In the years that followed, Lori taught me a lot about what people "out there" think about those of us "in here." She helped me see how weird and kind of scary church people look to people who, for whatever reason, are not part of a Christian faith community. We have a variety of rituals they don't totally understand (if at all!) and traditions that mean nothing to them. We speak a different language. What's worse, we don't always seem very interested in learning their language or finding out what is important to them.

But Lori also helped me realize that what we have—the good news of God's love for the world, through Jesus Christ—

is exactly what the world needs. This good news helped heal her. It gave her life a whole new direction. In all kinds of unexpected and wonderful ways, it set her free.

That summer, when I sat down to write, it was Lori's face I saw. In my imagination, she sat across the table from me as I wrote. I wanted, more than anything, to be able to help her hear the good news in a way that would make sense to her. And I wanted her to have the tools she would need to go deeper in her new faith.

A lot has happened since then.

Lori started reading the Bible. She learned to listen for God's voice. She dared to speak the words she heard God speaking. Now, Lori is a leader in the congregation. And together, she and I are part of a team that helps other congregations across the country share the good news with people in *their* communities.

More than ever, it is for people like Lori that I do what I do.

God is on a mission

It was so hard for me to leave that congregation, even for the opportunity to teach at a seminary. But many leaders in the congregation, including Lori, encouraged me to do it. I think they knew that to be the church means to be a part of God's mission to love and bless and save *the whole world*. To be sure, God loves and cares about us. God loves and cares about our congregations ... and our synods ... and our seminaries ... and our denomination. But God doesn't call us together to be the church for our own sakes. God's eyes are fixed on the world!

God loves the world. God loved it enough to send Jesus (read John 3:16). God created it! And it is a good, good world. But it is broken. And God will not stop until it is whole again. God is at work, right now, "reconciling the world to himself" (read 2 Corinthians 5:19).

You and I are invited to be a part of this adventure.

Yes, you.

Help wanted

Now, I know that if you were looking for a job right now, you could read the want ads in the newspaper or on a Web site, network with people who might be able to help with your search, and maybe even watch for "HELP WANTED" signs while you pound the pavement. But you wouldn't apply for every single job you found out about. Some jobs might sound a little boring to you. You might be overqualified for others. And some would require a license, degree, or training that you just don't have.

Well, this is a job that should never make you bored. It doesn't require certain qualifications, connections, or experience. If there was a want ad for this job, it might read like this:

Help wanted for the adventure of a lifetime. Benefits: a lifetime of adventure and more. On-the-job training. No experience necessary. Everybody's welcome!

Now, who wouldn't want a job like that? And you don't even need to apply for it. It's already yours! You see, God is on this amazing mission to love and bless and save the world. And God calls me—and you—to be a part of that adventure. I know it sounds weird but, for some reason, God wants our help. God loves us! And God wants our lives to make a difference. God wants our lives to *mean* something. So we've been hired for the job—to be a part of what God is up to in this world, to witness and serve and love and give ourselves away. We are God's partners in mission. That is our job, and God wants to put us to work.

On-the-job training

This is the main idea behind the new edition of this book. God is up to something! In fact, God has been up to something from the very beginning. Chapters 1 and 2 of this book say more about this mission and our partnership in it.

Maybe you're not sure you're quite up to the task. In fact, maybe the idea of being a part of God's mission in the world scares you half to death! Or, maybe you really are ready to finally get to work doing something that really matters. Or, just maybe, you've been at this work for a while and it's time for you to re-up, recommit, and reenergize. Here's some good news: There is on-the-job training available for all of us.

This book helps explain what it means to answer God's call to share the story of God's love with everybody (chapter 3), how we can hear God speak to us through the Bible (chapter 4), and the role of prayer in the Christian life (chapter 5). We'll explore the responsibility we have to serve people in need and share our stuff (chapter 6), and both the challenges and joys of living together as a community of faith (chapter 7).

All along the way, I'm hoping we'll learn and grow as partners in God's mission. We'll be reminded that when we mess things up (which happens a lot), God never, ever stops calling us back home again—and back to work. We'll be encouraged. We'll be challenged. And in many ways, we'll find ourselves being changed (chapter 8).

How to use this book

Maybe you're reading this book because you've never gone to a worship service or read anything in the Bible, and you don't know where to start. Maybe you used to go to church or read from the Bible, but that was a long time ago. Maybe you have some experience with the church, but reading and studying the Bible is kind of new to you. Or maybe you're an old hand. You've been at this for a long time. And God's mission is the greatest adventure you've ever been on. Well, everybody is welcome! I'm hoping that those with no experience will encounter a God who wants to speak to them in a way that makes sense to them. And I hope the very experienced will hear God speaking to them in a fresh, new way.

You can read this book on your own, of course. It's designed that way. But you might want to think about getting together with at least one or two others. Read each chapter and talk about your reactions to it, using the questions at the back of the book (pages 109-111). Learn from each other and encourage each other in the on-the-job training for your work in God's mission.

If you're in a small group using the No Experience Necessary Bible study series, talk about this book in your regular meetings or set up a special time to focus on this. The questions at the back of the book can jump-start your discussion.

No Experience Necessary Bible study series

The Bible is one very important way that God speaks to us today. The No Experience Necessary Bible study series is designed to encourage people to read directly from the Bible together, and then to talk about what they hear God saying to them. A No Experience Necessary small group can get going with as few as two or three people who want to learn from the Bible and each other. A congregation might start several groups at once or begin a No Experience Necessary Bible study with a group that already exists (for example, a new member class, a women's group, or a men's group). If there isn't a No Experience Necessary group for you to join, consider starting one yourself! Invite your neighbors, friends, coworkers, and family members— anybody who can't resist the idea that God wants to put them to work.

Climb aboard

God is up to something in this world, and has been since before time began! And so, you need to know that this great adventure is already in motion. If God's mission were a train, we would say it's already left the station. If it were a NASCAR race, everyone in the crowd would already be up on their feet, their cheering drowned out by the sound of screaming engines. If it were an important package being shipped across the world, you could log on and track its progress, only to find that it is already well on its way.

Being God's partner in the mission to love and bless and save the world is the adventure of a lifetime. And it brings a lifetime of adventure. To climb aboard or continue on this adventure, there's no experience necessary. That means no application. No interview. No waiting for the phone to ring. You're hired! Now it's time for on-the-job training. There's work to do.

A world full of people like Lori is waiting.

1 STRANGE, BUT WONDERFUL

The Bible can seem complicated and hard to
understand sometimes. It might help to know that
at the very center of this ancient book is this
wonderful truth: God loves us. In fact, no matter
how many times we try to run away from home,
God is willing to do whatever it takes to bring us
back again. And what's true for us is also true
for the world.

I have lost track of the number of people who tell me they
would like to read the Bible ... have tried to read the Bible ...
but just find it too hard to understand.

Among the people from whom I have heard this are teach-
ers and stockbrokers and nurses and farmers and, well, you
name it. Smart people. Successful people. Hardworking people.
All of them stumped by the Bible. And most of them feel alone.
Like they are the only ones in this predicament. The last place
they would ever go is to some Bible study or to a bookstore in
search of a Bible, because somebody might ask them something! And then they would have to reveal how little they
know.

Well, I'm not going to kid you. Reading the Bible really can
be hard work. There are people and places and stories of life
issues told there that are just totally unfamiliar to the average
reader today. We'll sort through some of that together later on.

But it can be surprisingly easy to read the Bible too. Sometimes, miraculously easy! Even in the beginning, you'll be reading along, and suddenly you'll get it. The truth will emerge as clearly as your reflection in the bathroom mirror as the steam from your shower is toweled away. In stunned silence, you know the words you have just read were meant for you.

It is not God's intention to keep the truth hidden from us. The Bible, after all, is the written account of what God has to say. God is actively trying to communicate with us through these words. And the single most important thing God is trying to say is this: you are loved.

Bob

The first time I realized how important—and how difficult—it is for us to understand the wonderful message at the center of the Bible came in the middle of my first month on the job. A handful of people were sitting around the table, most of them more scared than I was. They were sitting there because I was supposed to be teaching them about what it means to be a follower of Jesus. They were new members and, at that church, it was assumed that if you were a "new" one you couldn't possibly know as much as the "old" ones. So I was in the middle of talking about God's grace, which was where they told us in seminary we should always begin.

I was saying that grace works something like this: It's your first day of school. And you're nervous and shy and feeling completely inadequate. You're wondering whether or not you can cut it when suddenly the teacher walks in, looks you over, and says to the whole class, "You all get A's." Before you've done or said or accomplished or messed up anything! "Now," the teacher says with a smile, "just do your best." That, I told my class, is sort of what grace is like. God loves you before you even do anything to deserve it.

Now, I didn't make up this example of grace myself, although I can't remember where I first heard it. And it's not the best one I've ever used. In fact, it's really quite ordinary. But when I told that story this time, something wonderful happened.

I looked up across the table and I saw Bob. He was thirty-something, the owner of a moderately successful small business, the father of three. He actually had tears in his eyes. They were piling up on the rim of his eye and threatening to spill over right down his face. In public and all. "What's up, Bob?" I said in my blurt-it-out-and-hope-it-doesn't-backfire sort of way. And he said this: "I don't think I ever knew who God was before."

The heart of the matter

"I don't think I ever knew who God was."

It's amazing to me, although it shouldn't be, that for many people today those words are true. Like most of the people I know, I grew up thinking that God's job was to make life hard for us: "Do this" and especially "Don't do that." God took all the fun out of everything, we thought. God expects us to be perfect and is angry because we're not. In God's eyes, we'll never measure up.

Well that's just not how it works with God.

We know this because of Jesus (who, Christians believe, gives us the clearest picture there is of who God is and what God is up to). In the Bible, the people who mattered most to Jesus were the ones who needed him most. The messy. The ugly. The outsiders. It is still that way, I think. One day, while I was serving as pastor, I got a call from a guy who runs a group home for adults with disabilities. He asked if it would be okay for the residents of this home to come worship with us. I said, "Of course. But, why are you asking me?" He said, "Well, some congregations have said no."

It's easy to get mixed up. We figure, I guess, that if the world values something or someone, then God must value them too. And I guess we figure the opposite is also true. But Jesus wasn't like that. Not even close.

I think that's one of the reasons Jesus had so many people—sometimes thousands—following him wherever he went. He just wandered around the countryside issuing a simple invitation: "Follow me" (read Matthew 4:18-22). Along the way he picked up an unlikely group of followers and friends: fishermen, tax collectors, homemakers, and more.

Jesus has never been very choosy. He doesn't look for a diploma hanging on your wall. He doesn't care what your bank account balance is or even if your checkbook is balanced at all. He isn't interested in your wardrobe or your waistline or your annual winter vacation destination. Truth is, none of these things matter to Jesus.

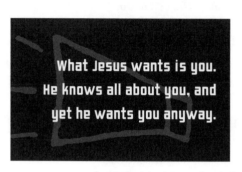

What Jesus wants is you. He knows all about you, and yet he wants you anyway.

What Jesus wants is you. He knows all about you, and yet he wants you anyway. Jesus knows about that test you cheated on in fourth grade. And that time you cheated on your taxes in 1983. And that time you were one drink away from cheating on your wife. He knows it all. And he wants you anyway. He wants me too. This is the heart of the matter, the number one truth of the Bible.

The "S" word

Jesus' mission and purpose are clear. When quizzed by the religious leaders of his day about what on earth he thought he was doing, Jesus explained it this way: He said he came for (brace yourself, now, I'm about to use the "S" word) … *sinners.*

Sin has gotten a bum rap in recent years. Self-help books and talk-show hosts encourage us to find the light within and just be our wonderful, true selves. Sin is a downer, they'll tell you. Describe yourself as a sinner and they'll tell you to find a good therapist. But the Bible tells us that Jesus chose to talk to sinners and forgive sin.

When Jesus said what he was up to, the religious leaders were upset that Jesus wasn't keeping all the rules. It was Jesus who broke the rule about not doing any work on the Sabbath. Sabbath is a holy day and, according to the religious law, it was a day to worship God and rest from all work. (The Sabbath was Saturday for Jesus, who grew up in the Jewish faith. For

Christians now, it's Sunday, the day of the week Jesus was raised from the dead.)

Anyway, Jesus did worship on the Sabbath. But when he showed up at the temple, there often would be people there who needed his help. And Jesus would help them. If they needed to be healed, he would heal them. This looked like work to the religious leaders, and it got Jesus into a lot of trouble. In fact, this is what made these religious leaders start working on a plot to have Jesus killed (read Mark 3:1-6).

It was in a confrontation with these religious leaders that Jesus used the "S" word.

He was having dinner with a pretty rough crowd one evening. Earlier that day, he had met a man named Levi. Levi was a tax collector, and not a nice man. Most people in town would have called him a thief and maybe even a traitor. They were Israelites. And Levi was working for Rome, the nation that was occupying their land at the time. But in spite of all that, Levi and Jesus hit it off. In fact, that day, Jesus issued a life-altering invitation to Levi, and Levi took him up on it. He left his work and his tax-collecting stand and followed Jesus. In his excitement, the first thing Levi did was open up the contact list in his PDA to call all his friends to invite them to a party where *they* could meet Jesus too. (Okay, maybe it didn't happen *exactly* like that!) But anyway, they came! Levi's house was full of unsavory characters and notorious bad guys. No respectable, law-abiding person in town would want this crowd in her or his living room. And, right there in the middle of them all sat Jesus, sharing jokes and eating cocktail weenies. And he loved those gathered with all his heart.

That's what made the religious leaders mad. They grabbed Jesus' disciples, his closest friends who went everywhere with him, and demanded, "Why is Jesus eating with such scum?! He knows it's wrong to eat with people who don't keep all the rules. *He's breaking the rules by doing it!*"

When Jesus heard about what the religious leaders had said, he went looking for them. When Jesus found them, he said something like this: "Look, I know this might be hard for you to understand. But these are exactly the people I came here for. I came for all those who are sick and in trouble and have lost their way. I came to invite sinners." (This story is so important that it's told in three places in the Bible. Read Mark 2:13-17; as well as Matthew 9:9-13; Luke 5:27-32.)

Jesus helped us understand, you see, that being a *sinner* is not necessarily about breaking the rules. (In fact, sometimes following Jesus means that, if a rule is unjust or unhelpful, you *have* to break it.) In reality, sin isn't much about rules at all. Sin is about breaking our relationship with God. And that is something we *all* do, you and I and even those rule-obsessed religious leaders. Sin is about trying to go our own way, without caring what God has to say. Sin is like telling God, "I don't need you! I can do this on my own!" It is, in a way, a lot like running away from home, again and again, no matter how much trouble we get ourselves or others into. (Read Luke 15:11-32 for a story about a young man who did this!) And God's heart hurts when that happens.

God's heart aches

I got my first clear picture of what this looks like from a baseball. It was a baseball that gave my little brother his first concussion. A baseball gave me my first lesson in life's injustices: they wouldn't let me play on a real team because I was a girl. No matter that my pitching arm was the best in the neighborhood. I was also a pretty good hitter, which is how we got in so much trouble that day.

My brother threw it. And I hit it ... right through his bedroom window. My dad was surprisingly calm about the whole thing. He brought the ball out into the yard, having recovered it from wherever it landed. We didn't actually see where it landed because we were hiding behind the garage praying for the power of invisibility. When our dad found us, he gave us the ball back and asked us not to play baseball in the yard anymore. It was a pretty small yard and we were getting a lot better at the game. We took the ball. Dad went to the hardware store. The window was fixed by suppertime.

What happened the next day is not quite as clear. There was that same troublesome little ball, lying in the middle of a pile of glass, in the middle of my brother's bedroom, having smashed its way through the very same window for the *second* time in two days. Dumb, I know. This time my dad was in the backyard, spherical evidence in hand, before we could even take cover. I said it was my brother's fault. He blamed me. My dad didn't seem to care. He sent us to our rooms. To wait.

I was only about eight years old at the time, but every second of my short life flashed before my eyes as I sat on my bed and waited for my dad's wrath to descend upon me. I deserved every bit of it. And I knew it.

My dad must have seen the guilt written all over my face. He had come in to deliver a spanking. (We know now this isn't exactly the most effective disciplinary technique, but back then it was pretty much standard operating procedure for lots of parents.) At any rate, it never got past the token stage. And he even had a hard time doing that. With the saddest eyes I think I've ever seen, my dad said, "This hurts me more than it hurts you."

In that moment, I didn't exactly believe him. But then I had kids of my own. Kids who—as wonderful as they are and as hard as we've tried to help them avoid it—have made their share of mistakes and will make plenty more. And now I know what my dad was talking about. It really *does* hurt us when we see our kids messing up.

It hurts most when we can't fix it for them, the way we could when a Band-Aid would do the trick. It is a terrible thing to have to watch as our kids answer for their mistakes, to have to stand by as they endure consequences they might otherwise have been able to avoid. We hurt for our kids even *before* they get hurt because we can anticipate the trouble they're in for. Our kids don't usually understand the seriousness of their actions. They have no idea. But we do. We can see it coming. It's as clear to us as ... well ... as clear as that brand new window was the second time my dad replaced it.

Back home again

That's how it works for God. God can see the trouble we get into and hurt we cause, the wars we start, the hearts we break, and the air we pollute. God can see the way a few of us hoard the wealth in the world and send way too many people to bed hungry. God can see the lines we draw to keep other people on the edges of life, victims of intolerance and prejudice. God can see that sometimes we find *ourselves* on the wrong side of those lines, out of luck and out in the cold. God can see the despair in our eyes, the blood on our hands, and the mess this good creation has become. And, so, God sent Jesus to make things right.

Jesus came into this world as *the living expression* of God's aching heart. This was God's answer to our trouble-making, relationship-breaking sinfulness. This was God's response to our cries for help. Jesus burst onto the scene announcing that, from now on, everything would be different. "The kingdom of God has come near," Jesus declared. "Repent, and believe in the good news." This is how Jesus starts his ministry in Galilee (read Mark 1:15). In other words, know that all of it is for you! Then Jesus spent the rest of his life showing us exactly what this all meant.

Jesus healed the sick and confronted the forces of evil. He welcomed people no one else would. He forgave the unforgivable. He erased the lines we had drawn to separate us from each other. Jesus saw the good in people and helped them see what they were good for. He challenged the most oppressive aspects of his culture. He made it clear that no government and no religious authority are above God. Jesus wept at the sight of our suffering. He gave hope to the hopeless. He brought the dead back to life. Jesus came to love.

In Jesus we have the clearest picture of who God is and what God is up to. And nowhere is this clearer than on the cross. There on the cross, we see a God who will stop at nothing to save us, a God who will give everything there is to give in order to reach us. This is a strange God, to be sure. I mean, which one of us could explain why God would choose to do things this way? Strange, but wonderful.

The very last thing Jesus did, the day he died on that cross, was to reach out and save someone (read Luke 23:39-43). At least two others were put to death beside him that awful day. They were criminals. And according to one of them, anyway, whatever he had done had earned him this death sentence. He had made a real mess of everything. He knew it. And he didn't think he had any right to expect mercy but he was scared. So he cried out for help. "Remember me when you come into your kingdom" (Luke 23:42). He wouldn't have dared to ask Jesus to *take* him there. He knew he was too much of a sinner for that. But God loves sinners. Jesus replied, "Today you will be with me in Paradise" (Luke 23:43). Another way to put it: today, you're coming with me.

God is on a mission

In Jesus, we meet a God on a mission. God created this world. Everyone and everything in it belongs to God. God knows what a mess we make of it. But God is determined to see it made holy and whole again. That is what Jesus came to tell us. That's what Jesus came to *do*. To rescue those who know that without him they don't stand a chance. To make things right for a world full of people who have done their best to make things wrong. To fix it when we have wronged each other. To chase down the runaways. To bring us all back home again.

"Here's the deal," Jesus so much as said. "Let's say you have a hundred sheep. And one of them gets lost. What would you do? You'd leave behind the ones who were safely tucked into the fold and go look for the lost sheep until you found it, right? And when you found it, you'd be so glad you'd throw it over your shoulders and carry it home." (You can read this story in Luke 15:1-7.)

That's what Jesus was all about. Because of him, we know that this is what our strange and wonderful God is all about.

There are a lot of things in the Bible that can be hard to understand. Sometimes the story is difficult to follow. But at the heart of it is this simple message: Before we can do a single thing to help or prove or defend ourselves, God plants an A+ right on our foreheads and right on our hearts. And when we're in a mess, whether or not it is a mess of our own making, God will do whatever it takes to make things right. God loves us. As Bob now knows, that's just who God is.

Where (in what place, situation, or relationship) do you think God might be calling you to make a difference?

Pray for

For God so loved the world that he gave his only Son, so that everyone who believes in him may not perish but may have eternal life.

John 3:16

2 | THE ADVENTURE OF A LIFETIME

God is on a mission to bless the world and bring it back home—holy and whole. Oddly enough, God wants our help. We are called to be partners with God in this amazing adventure. Answering that call is what gives our lives real purpose and meaning.

I am enough a child of the 1970s to remember the days when searching for the "meaning of life" wasn't the weirdest thing a person could do. The Beatles did it. A lot of people did. Great pilgrimages were made to visit wise and distant gurus. College professors, at least a few famous ones, extolled the wonders of chemically induced visions and insights. In other words, they encouraged people to get high and get in tune with the universe. And parents all over the country scratched their heads as their twenty-something children took off to "find themselves" for a while.

I can't say that anybody in my neighborhood went looking for the meaning of life. They were all too busy trying to pay the rent or make mortgage payments, and to put food on the table for their kids. But I'm guessing even they wondered, every once in a while, what the point of it all is.

I'm thinking that, at one time or another, we all do.

Wise words

The Bible tells us that King Solomon was the wisest, richest man in the history of Israel. And yet, he's the guy who is said to have written "Vanity of vanities! All is vanity" (Ecclesiastes 1:2). The New Living Translation puts it this way: "Everything is meaningless ... utterly meaningless!" Both of these are ways of asking, "What's the point?!"

What do we get in return for our work? Solomon went on. Time passes, but things don't change. And it doesn't matter what we do, we just aren't satisfied. Solomon tried everything to fill the emptiness in his life. He pursued things that amused him. He drank himself silly. He built huge homes and planted beautiful vineyards. He bought slaves and herds and flocks, more than any king who had ever lived before. He collected piles of silver and gold. He hired people to sing and dance for him. He had any woman he wanted.

He even tried hard work!

Then Solomon looked at what he had done and realized it was all for nothing, "a chasing after wind" (Ecclesiastes 2:11). None of it meant anything.

In the end, Solomon came to some interesting conclusions. (He wasn't known as the wisest person in the world for nothing.) He decided that the things we do in this life only *really* mean something if they are connected to what God is doing. Enjoy the good things in life, he said. Work hard. Search for wisdom. Be generous. Tend to your relationships. But never, ever forget that you and everything you have belongs to the Lord. And above all, "fear God, and keep his commandments" (Ecclesiastes 12:13).

The point is, of course, that people don't live on bread alone. There is more to life than making a living. And when we get ourselves stuck there, thinking that more "stuff" is what matters more than anything else, we end up miserable.

As far back as the 1830s, Alexis de Tocqueville, a French politician who visited the United States, said that Americans were especially vulnerable to this danger because of their potential to have so much more stuff than anybody else. What's the best protection we have against this danger? Back then, Tocqueville said, the best thing Americans had going for them was their religion. They had their eyes on something other than their stuff. Their attention was turned to heaven. (Read Tocqueville's observations for yourself in his famous book *Democracy in America*.)

You probably haven't visited a mountaintop guru lately to ask about the "meaning of life." If you tried searching the Internet for it, maybe late one night in a half-joking, half-desperate moment, you would find more than 24 million links taking you mostly nowhere. Now, I'm not saying you won't find anything helpful out there, on the Web or in a bookstore or on a daytime talk show.

But I can tell you this. Nothing you do or earn or accomplish or create will mean anything unless it's connected to what God is doing.

And God is on a mission to bless the world.

A weird twist

As we've seen, Jesus gives us the clearest picture of what this mission looks like. God wants love to rule the day! God wants to see enemies become friends and hungry people filled up. God wants the walls we have built up between people of different languages and cultures and generations and lifestyles torn down. God wants the earth to be cleaned up, and wars to end, and everyone everywhere to know the God who loves them. God wants us to be free of whatever it is that tears us down and holds us back from being everything we have been created to be. God wants us to have *real* life, not the fake one so many of us are living. When Jesus gave his life so that all of these things could happen, he showed us just how serious God is about this mission. Nothing—not even the forces of evil or the power of death—can stop it.

But maybe the weirdest thing about this mission is that God uses people like us to get it done. God wants our help.

When Jesus showed up, he didn't leave us guessing about the mission God had sent him on. "I must proclaim the good news of the kingdom of God to the other cities also; for I was sent for this purpose" (Luke 4:43). And then, the very next thing he did was to go out and find some people to help him.

Jesus was preaching on the shore of the Sea of Galilee, with a big crowd all around, when he saw a couple of empty boats not far away. The fishermen were bummed out because they had been out all night with no fish to show for it. They were busy cleaning their nets, and getting ready to go home for breakfast and a nap, when Jesus went over and climbed into one of the boats. I don't know this for sure, but I'm thinking the fishermen were probably a little annoyed when Jesus asked them to take him out onto the water so the crowd could see and hear him better. And I'm guessing they were even more annoyed when, after he was done teaching, he told them to take him fishing.

One of the fishermen was named Simon Peter (whom Jesus named Peter). "Master," he said, "we have worked all night long but have caught nothing" (Luke 5:5).

But he did what Jesus asked anyway. He put his nets down, right where Jesus told him to, and couldn't believe it when he pulled them back up again. They were so full of fish the nets began to tear. Simon Peter shouted to his friends to come and help, which they did. (They were probably a lot less annoyed now.)

Simon Peter knew he was in the presence of someone like no one he had ever met before. He fell to his knees before Jesus and said, "Go away from me, Lord, for I am a sinful man!" (Luke 5:8).

But Jesus wouldn't hear of it. "Do not be afraid!" Jesus said, "from now on you will be catching people" (Luke 5:10).

The story in Luke tells us that, as soon as they got back to shore, Simon Peter and the others "left everything" to follow Jesus (Luke 5:11). But the story doesn't tell us why. Maybe they felt sick and tired of their day jobs (especially given the way things had been going lately) and were ready for something new. Maybe they figured their nets would always be full if they stuck close to Jesus. Maybe they were just curious.

Maybe.

But here's my guess. I think that, somehow, they knew this call to follow Jesus was the greatest gift they would ever receive.

A new job

"The church is a hospital for sinners." Maybe you've heard the church described this way before. I've heard it from a lot of different people over the years, and I heard it again just the other day.

I think that's wrong.

Oh, I know we're sinners, all right. (See chapter 1 again, in case you need a quick refresher.) And it's not bad to be reminded that the church is full of them—I mean, us. But comparing the church to a hospital just doesn't work for me.

Have you ever been in a hospital? I was, twice. And both times I wasn't what you'd call sick. (Tired, yes, after labor. But not sick.) Even so, I didn't exactly pull my weight at the hospital while I was there. I wasn't up cleaning bedpans or administering IVs or saying, "Scalpel, please," in that confident doctor voice. I just laid there while everybody else around me did the work. They were the experts, after all. This was their territory. My place was in bed, watching the soaps and looking forward to the red gelatin I ordered for dinner. And it never occurred to me that it should be any other way.

Now, unfortunately, I know that a lot of congregations look a little something like that, with most of the people observing while "experts" do the ministry. But I don't believe this is what Jesus intends.

I have a friend who is somewhat new to the faith. He became part of a congregation I was serving, shortly after we opened the doors of a new ministry center. A couple of months after he and his family started worshiping with us, his wife and four children were baptized. He is a very busy guy, the head chef at a restaurant. And he did what he could in terms of getting involved in the work of the congregation. But very early on he came to see *everything* he did as ministry. For example, at work he makes a point of knowing all the dishwashers in his kitchen. He asks them about their families. He treats them like coworkers. He cares about them. He knows he is responsible to do more than make really good food. He has been put in the restaurant by God to make a difference in the lives of the people who work with him. Anyway, this friend of mine will tell you that one of the first things he learned after he started coming to worship was this: When you meet Jesus, you get a job.

And his smile will be big as day when he tells you this.

Because, here's the truth: Having just about *any* job can make you feel worthwhile. Being given a job by Jesus is a gift beyond words.

An undeserved call

Jesus' call to us is a gift, first of all, because it is so completely undeserved and unearned. I mean, we're talking about Jesus here—God's only Son, the long awaited Messiah, the King of kings, and the Lord of lords. Can you honestly think of one good reason for Jesus to pick Simon Peter and the rest of his unlucky (or untalented!) fishing buddies?

Frankly, I don't think there is one good reason for Jesus to pick *us*, either. Not that you and I are without talent or imagination or skill. We all bring along something helpful on this adventure. But Jesus knows there is more to us than the best face and the good manners we put on when company's over. Jesus knows all about us. ALL about us. He knows stuff about you and me that we don't even want to admit to ourselves. And yes, he knows we're not perfect. He's not the least bit surprised when we mess things up along the way. He knew we would the moment he laid eyes on us.

"Peter, you're going to run away when the going gets tough," Jesus basically said in the final days before his arrest. "Really. You all will."

And sure enough, as soon as the soldiers hauled Jesus away, Jesus' followers all scattered. Simon Peter hung on longer than the rest of them, following Jesus to the site of his trial. But he stayed hidden in the shadows and, as soon as somebody recognized him, he caved.

"I don't know what you're talking about," the terrified disciple said. "I don't even know the guy. I swear I don't." (Read the story in Mark 14.)

This was terrible and tragic, and Peter probably felt miserable as soon as he did it. But Jesus knew this would happen, one way or another, all along. Jesus knows our every failure, our every fault. Jesus knows we'll fall. And he wants us anyway. He *calls* us anyway. One moment we're washing out our nets, minding our own ordinary business, and the next moment Jesus shows up.

"Hey, you," he says.

"Who, me?" you ask.

"Yes, you." He smiles. And in that smile, you see everything. You see how much he loves you. And you see how little you deserve it.

"Come follow me."

A call that changes everything

This call from Jesus is the most wonderful *gift* you will ever get. Why is the call a gift? First of all, it is utterly undeserved. Second, it will change your life more than anything else that will ever happen to you.

When Jesus calls us to follow him, he invites us to come and be a part of the biggest adventure ever. Jesus was sent by God, remember? And God is on a mission to bless and save and love the whole world. There is nothing going on anywhere on the planet that is more important than this. This is the only real game in town. And make no mistake, this is God's game. God is willing to give everything to see this mission fulfilled. This broken world *will* be put back together again. Every broken life *will* be made whole. God *will* see this done. That's what God is up to. In fact, this is what God has been up to since before time began. In some ways, God's mission is like a train that has already left the station. And when Jesus calls us to be a part of this, it's like getting a ticket to ride.

Let me tell you, coming to understand this has made all the difference in my own life.

My first real job after I graduated from college (not counting the one week of telemarketing, the two weeks as a bank teller, and the three months of muffin baking–don't ask) was working for an organization committed to economic justice, environmental protection, and social change. The folks in this organization did really good work. At first, I loved this job.

I went door-to-door in one Long Island neighborhood after another, informing people about the work that was going on and inviting them to participate by giving a donation, signing petitions, and writing letters. (Does this sound scary? It was a blast! And the best preparation I could have had for planting a congregation.) We actually accomplished a lot of really important things. But after a short time, I just couldn't take it anymore. I was glad when another job opportunity came along, and I could quit with a clear conscience. You see, the people I was working with in this organization were just too ... I don't know ... optimistic. They actually thought they were going to change the world. And I knew better. I knew that, no matter how many little victories we might win along the way, THE WORLD IS JUST MORE MESSED UP THAN WE CAN HANDLE. There would always be more poverty, more pollution, more racism, and more PROBLEMS than we could ever fix. No matter *how hard* we worked. And in the end, the whole project just made me depressed.

Well, that is bound to happen every time we think WE can change the world. This is what happens every time we make the mistake of thinking that OUR projects, whatever they are, really mean something. Solomon was a pretty smart guy, after all.

Now I know the truth. *My* project isn't going to change the world at all. And *my* work, no matter how noble or important it is, isn't going to make the difference. God's project, on the other hand, is already changing everything. Right now, today, God is setting people free. God is filling the ears of people who are poor with good news–and often even filling their stomachs.

God is healing the wounds we have inflicted upon each other and the relationships we have tried to destroy. God is bringing light into even the darkest places.

God is creating faith communities of radical love where everyone really is welcome, no matter how discriminated against or despised they might be in society (and, too often, even in the church). God is creating new life, even in those places where death seems to have won the day. God is doing these things in our homes, our schools, our workplaces, our congregations, our communities, the church, and across all the nations of the world.

> The train has already left the station. God is on the move. "Come follow me," Jesus says, which really means, "Hop aboard!"

That is a project I want to be a part of. That is the mission Jesus invites me to help carry out. That is my call. And it's your call too. The outcome doesn't depend on our efforts. God will see that this mission gets done. That's why we can give ourselves to it with all our hearts and minds and souls. We can work tirelessly for the causes we believe in, generously give away our money, and dedicate ourselves to doing the right thing at work and in our relationships. We can speak up for people who have no voice even when it's dangerous, care for the earth even when it's inconvenient, and invite others into a relationship with Jesus Christ even when the very thought of doing that scares us half to death.

And we can do these things with absolute confidence that, because this is God's gig, our efforts will make a difference. Our lives will *mean something*.

No wonder Peter left his boats behind. He would never get a greater gift than the one he got the day Jesus called him.

Looking ahead

When I was growing up, the folks in my neighborhood didn't have time or patience for a lot of navel gazing. My dad, for example, worked two or three jobs just to pay the bills. Around the house, we did anything that had to be done.

We fixed it or cleaned it or tore it down or replaced it. There was no money to pay somebody else to do those things for us. That's how life was for everybody. About the only time I remember my parents just kicking back and relaxing was on Sunday afternoons, when the whole family would gather at my great-grandparents' home for dinner and card games and conversation. In the evening, everybody would gather around the TV (they *had* one!) to watch Lawrence Welk and his orchestra. There was a lot of laughter on those long, lazy Sundays. They were respites from the rest of life. No one would have thought to pipe up in the middle of it all with a question like this: "So does anybody here have *any* idea what the meaning of life is?" That would have been a conversation-stopper, for sure. After a moment, maybe somebody would have laughed—sure, they got the joke. And my grandmother would have taken that as her cue to say, "Pie, anyone?"

But I'm a grown-up now. And I know a lot more about the people who sat around that table. I've heard their stories and all the stories about them. I've seen their scars. And I don't have any doubt that, in their own way, each one of them asked the "meaning of life" question at one time or another. Some of them were more successful at figuring out an answer than others. A few chased the question, for a long time, in some pretty self-destructive ways. In at least one case, the failure to answer it led to utter despair and an early, awful death.

I don't care who you are or what you do for a living or how goofy you might think those Beatles were, each one of us needs to know that our time on this planet makes a difference. We need to feel like there is some purpose we are meant to fulfill. We need to know that our lives matter.

In the meantime, the train has already left the station. God is on the move. "Come follow me," Jesus says, which really means, "Hop aboard!" It is there (and I believe *only* there) as we participate in God's mission to bless and love the world, that we will find answers to our deepest questions.

We can spend ourselves in the effort to build healthy relationships and raise faithful children. We can exhaust ourselves trying to create communities where every person is valued and no one goes hungry. We can commit ourselves to conducting our business with integrity and resisting every temptation to do otherwise. We can do our best to overcome every fear to invite everyone we meet into a life of faith. We can dedicate ourselves to protecting the earth's resources. And maybe we'll look back at the end of our lives and say, "Well, we did some good." But when we know that our efforts—even the smallest ones—are all a part of God's mission in this world, we won't look back at all. We'll look ahead, into the future that God is already bringing in. And we'll see that, all along, we were on the adventure of a lifetime.

God has been using us to change the world.

One dishwasher at a time.

 **Where (in what place, situation, or relationship) do you think God might be calling you to make a difference?**

Pray for

Jesus said to Simon, "Do not be afraid; from now on you will be catching people."
Luke 5:10

3 | A LIFETIME OF ADVENTURE

Our lives take on new meaning as we follow God into adventure. God has plans for us. The main job we've been given is to share the story of God's love with everybody, in our words and through our actions.

W ell, so far, so good. The God who loves and forgives us is on a mission to love and bless and save the whole world. Most amazing of all, God wants our help with this mission! God invites us all to be a part of this adventure. This call, which we haven't done anything to deserve, is a gift. And it gives our lives the meaning and purpose we all need so much.

But to simply say the call is a gift is just half of the story.

The truth is, the gift God gives to us through Jesus Christ is also a call.

Now, I'm not very good at beating around the bush, so I'll just spit this out and hope I don't offend too many people.  It seems to me that there are way too many anemic Christians walking around today. Actually, they're mostly sitting around. They have this idea that being a Christian is about *going to church*. They think church is where you confess your sins (usually along with a whole bunch of other people who are confessing their sins at the same time, so it feels like, if you're lucky, God might not even notice) and have them forgiven (whew), listen to a (hopefully) good sermon that will give you something to think about during the week, get Communion (and that extra boost of God it gives), and go home ready to endure another week of life (which, let's face it, can be a drag a lot of the time).

I'll be honest and say that, for a big part of my life, that's what I thought being a Christian was all about.

There are only two problems with that scenario.

Stop *going* to church

First of all, being a Christian isn't about *going* to church.

It's about *being* the church.

Imagine for a minute what the church looked like when it first got started. (You can read all about this for yourself in the Bible, in the book of Acts.) There weren't any pastors with seminary training, because there weren't any seminaries. There weren't any Bibles, but the early Christians, who came from the Jewish faith, did have Scriptures—the law and the prophets— which we now include in our "Old Testament." The "New Testament" wasn't written yet—that means no written stories about Jesus, no letters from Paul, no weird book of Revelation, *nothing*. There weren't even any church buildings. The point is that early Christians couldn't go to church because *there was no "church" to go to.* The early believers knew the church isn't a pastor or a book (not even a really GOOD book) or a building. There was no room for confusion. They knew that *the church is people.* Now, these people had heard the call of Jesus and been given the gift of the Holy Spirit. (It's all there in Acts 1 and 2.) They weren't just *any* bunch of people. But they were, finally, ordinary *people.*

Those of us who are heirs of the sixteenth-century Protestant Reformation (including Lutherans) really shouldn't be confused about this. Martin Luther himself once said, "God be praised, a seven-year-old child knows what the church is: holy believers and 'the little sheep who heard the voice of their shepherd'" (*Smalcald Articles*, Article 12: Concerning the Church, *The Book of Concord*, Augsburg Fortress, 2000, pp. 324-325).

In other words, the church is *people* who are listening to and following Jesus together. (Luther said this, by the way, because too many people in his day thought the church was defined by fancy robes and rituals done by pastors. I'm serious. Look it up yourself.)

So what does all this mean? We don't *go* to church. We *are* the church. We are the church in our workplaces and in our schools, in our homes and at the skate park, at the mall and at the gym, at the bus stop, and at the beauty shop. Once a week or so we get together to share a Meal, to hear from each other, and to learn from God's Word. Jesus shows up in those gatherings, reminding us that our sins are forgiven and sending us out again to be the church "out there." We need these weekly get-togethers. Being the church out there is hard! In fact, many of us gather more often than once a week. We get together in small groups and social groups and prayer groups to study, and to serve, and to share our lives. But the point of all this "gathering" isn't the gathering. The point is the "going." In the gathering, we are encouraged and challenged and equipped for the life we are called to live *as the church* out there.

A lot of Christians suffering from anemia need a boost of iron. We need to be reminded that being a Christian isn't about going to church at all. It's about *being* church.

The gift is a call

The second thing a lot of Christians are confused about is this: We don't "get" God and all of God's blessings for ourselves and our own sake. God blesses us so that, through us, others will be blessed.

In other words, the gifts that God gives come with a call.

Now, I know this might seem like a strange idea. A gift is a *gift*, right? No strings attached! That's right. But it is also true that it is the nature of some gifts to bring with them enormous *responsibilities*. God's gifts are like that.

And just in case you're not sure about this, let a seven-year-old explain this one, too.

When I was about seven or eight years old, I got the Christmas present every kid dreams of. My dad, who had sworn he'd never do this, broke down and brought a puppy home. He was just a mutt from the pound, which may be why Dad fell in love with him.

I don't know where Dad kept the little guy until Christmas Eve. But that night, after my brother and I were asleep, he snuck the puppy into our house and put a big bow around his neck. Then Dad set up a little bed for the puppy under a table in the living room, near the Christmas tree. He tucked the puppy in, presumably for the night, and headed off to bed himself.

Only Santa knows what happened next.

The next morning, my brother and I were up at the first hint of daylight, racing each other to the pile of presents we were expecting under the tree. What we found was a pile, all right. There was shredded wrapping paper and scattered ribbon everywhere. I don't remember all the details anymore but let's just say most of our presents came to us that morning "slightly used." Someone had clearly played with them before we had. Correction—it looked like someone had tried to eat them. We were stunned. Horrified. It was like the Grinch himself, unsatisfied by his midnight demolition of Whoville, had visited our humble home.

Our mad dash through the house hadn't managed to shake our parents from sleep, but the sudden silence did. They came stumbling out into the living room, their sleepy but expectant smiles quickly disappearing at the sight of us. We must have been a pathetic pair. My dad, though, knew just what would turn this situation around. A smile quietly crept back onto his face. "So, have you met our little visitor yet?" he asked us mysteriously.

It took us a minute. My brother and I looked at each other and back again at Dad's goofy grin. Then we looked around. Past the tangle of slightly chewed Barbie dolls and board games. Past the ornaments that littered the floor, and the undone lights hanging askew from every Christmas tree branch. Past our knowing parents.

Finally, we were able to see the puddles. Puddles, puddles everywhere! There was some kind of creature somewhere in that house, who clearly had a bit too much excitement during the night. After a lively hunt, we found the mischievous mongrel, sound asleep beneath a chair.

A family meeting was called to order. A vote was taken. Our new best friend's name? What else but ... *Puddles*.

This was my first introduction to the idea that some gifts bring along with them enormous responsibilities.

Pack up your things

As a matter of fact, this is one of the first lessons the Bible teaches us. In the book of Genesis, we meet a couple named Abraham and Sarah. These two received one of the most amazing gifts ever given. But they soon came to realize the great responsibility that went along with the gift.

Abraham and Sarah had made a comfortable life for themselves, surrounded by family and friends in Haran, where Abraham had been born. Sarah was unable to have children of her own. And because of the times they lived in, thousands of years before Jesus was even around, this was not only an unbearable disappointment to her. It was seen as a disgrace.

Somehow, though, Abraham and Sarah had managed to survive it all and he was now seventy-five years old. Then one day, God showed up. "Abraham," God said, "today is your lucky day." (Read the whole story in Genesis 12.)

The Bible doesn't tell us how Abraham responded to this. Moses was amazed and afraid when God spoke to him at the burning bush (Exodus 3:1-6) and later the people were so terrified when they realized God was on the mountaintop that they pleaded with Moses not to let God speak to them too (Exodus 20:18-19). In New Testament times, just about every time angels appeared with a message from God the first thing they said was, "Don't be afraid!" because they knew people were scared silly at the sight of them. (Read Luke 1:13, 29-30, for example.) But Abraham? Maybe he was just too stunned to be scared.

"Pack up your things," God said to Abraham. "I've got plans for you." A great adventure waited for Abraham and Sarah beyond Haran. "Follow me," God said, "and I'll show you a new land. And there, I will bless you with every single thing you have ever hoped for." God promised to make Abraham and Sarah famous, powerful, and wealthy beyond their dreams. God told Abraham that he would be the "father of a great nation," which was the strangest thing of all because, at that point, Abraham hadn't even fathered a child.

Now let's be clear about one thing before we go any further. Because these two were biblical characters and all, you might be thinking they somehow deserved all this attention.

> The gifts God gave to Abraham and Sarah were intended to bless everyone, everywhere, of every time and every place.

You might even be used to thinking that if somebody is in the Bible, they had to be at least *a little* more holy than the rest of us. Well, if you look closely you'll find that the people we read about in the Bible, except for Jesus, of course, weren't one bit more saintly than any of the rest of us. (Even the disciples, as we've seen, were a mixed bag.) And there isn't anything, according to this story, that tells us Abraham and Sarah had done something to deserve all of these special favors. They were probably nice enough people. But the story doesn't say Abraham and Sarah were *especially* nice, or honest or generous or faithful or anything else. We aren't told anywhere that Abraham and Sarah *deserved* these gifts from God. In fact, as the story unfolds, we discover that Abraham and Sarah messed up and made bad choices and rebelled against God's wishes just as often as any of us do. So it's absolutely clear: The blessings God promised to shower upon Abraham and Sarah were in fact *gifts*.

But these gifts came with (all together, now!) enormous responsibility.

God told Abraham and Sarah that they were being blessed this way so that, through them, God could bless others. In fact, God said, "In you all the families of the earth shall be blessed" (Genesis 12:3). All the families of the earth! The gifts God gave to Abraham and Sarah were intended to bless everyone, everywhere, of every time and every place. God's plan was to work through Abraham and Sarah, and their descendants, to bring the whole world back home again.

Abraham and Sarah are remembered now as the father and mother of the Israelite people. And sometimes these people are called "the chosen people." It's true. They were chosen. But it wasn't because of anything they had done to deserve it. It was because God was on a mission to love and bless the world. And they were the people through whom God chose to do it.

The gift that God gave to Abraham and Sarah was also a call. That's how it works for us too.

Bridge building 101

Picture this: There is a bowl of water, various family members and friends, a smiling and patient congregation, and a baby. Parents solemnly promise to pray for this little one and to teach her how to pray. They say they will raise her up to know and love God, and they commit themselves to providing the best example they can of what it means to follow Jesus. Sponsors do the same. Finally, the splash: "I baptize you in the name of the Father, and of the Son, and of the Holy Spirit." Marked with the cross of Christ forever. Everyone applauds. The parents smile nervously, feeling the magnitude of their promises. Grandparents, clicking one photo after another, silently vow to do everything they can to help.

The baby sleeps or cries through the whole thing.

The point is, all of these remarkable events have transpired and the baby wasn't aware of any of it. Totally oblivious, this little one has received the gift of baptism, God's big wet sloppy kiss, and a promise that nothing in all creation will ever be able to separate her from God's love. She hasn't had to earn it. It was given to her before she could say or do anything to deserve it. It is a gift made possible through the life and death and resurrection of Jesus Christ. She has been blessed beyond imagination, beyond reason.

What she doesn't know yet, but will hopefully one day discover, is that this gift she has received is also a call. She has been blessed so that she can be a blessing to others.

She has been called to be a part of God's mission in the world. So have I. And so have you.

Here's how the Bible says it: "You are a chosen race, a royal priesthood, a holy nation, God's own people, in order that you may proclaim the mighty acts of him who called you out of darkness into his marvelous light" (1 Peter 2:9).

When we are welcomed into the community of faith, we become *priests*. Every single one of us. And that means it is our job to be "go-betweens"—between people and God. We're like a bridge God uses to reach people. (In fact, the Latin word for *priest* means "bridge builder"!)

So that …

Our relationship with God should not put us to sleep. When Jesus stretched out his arms on the cross to embrace us and this whole messed-up world we live in, he didn't do it so that we could go home and take a nap. He didn't even do it so that we could go to church and be benchwarmers.

Paul, the famous letter writer and early Christian missionary, wrote to his friends: "[Christ] died for all, so that those who live might live no longer for themselves, but for him who died and was raised for them" (2 Corinthians 5:15). Read all of 2 Corinthians 5 for a clear picture of how this whole thing works.

And how do we live for Christ? Again, here's how Paul puts it: "All this is from God, who reconciled us to himself through Christ, and has given us the ministry of reconciliation; that is, in Christ God was reconciling the world to himself, not counting their trespasses against them, and entrusting the message of reconciliation to us" (2 Corinthians 5:18-19).

When God comforts us, it is *so that* we can be a comfort to others. When God encourages us, it is *so that* we can be an encouragement to others. When God saves us, it is *so that* others can be saved. Read through Paul's letters and count how many times he says "so that" or "therefore." Or just check out 2 Corinthians 1:3-7. God fills up our ears and our hearts and our lives with good news *so that* we can share that news with everyone.

Martin Luther put it this way. He said that, through Christ, we are set free from sin, death, and the devil (in other words, anything that would kill us if it could) *so that* we are free to serve Christ and our neighbor. He said this in 1520 in an important little booklet called *The Freedom of a Christian*, and his own life was an example of how this works.

Luther grew up in Germany, in a time when there were all kinds of superstitions about God floating around. It was easy to get mixed up. The Bible was still in Latin at that time, and there was hardly anyone who could understand it, including many of the priests. Most people couldn't read at all. On top of that, life was hard back then, even for wealthy people. There was sickness and plague. Death came early and, for many, was a relief. Living such a cruel life, it wasn't a stretch to imagine a cruel God. People in Luther's day were afraid of God. And they were terrified of eternity.

The church responded. You can be sure of heaven, the church taught, if you just give enough money or go on enough long pilgrimages (searching for holy relics or performing other holy deeds) or keep the right spiritual disciplines strictly enough. Luther totally bought into this whole thing.

And then he read the Bible.

In the pages of John's Gospel, the words of the psalms, and the writings of Paul, Martin Luther discovered a God unlike anything he had encountered before. Luther discovered a God who loved him and sent Jesus, as a gift, to save him and set him free. His life was never the same after that. He was like a crazy man, spending himself in the effort to make sure everyone had the opportunity to meet the same wonderful God. He translated the Bible into German so everyone in his country could read it. He wrote booklets, even for children, that explained the basic truths of the Bible. He wrote songs, using popular and familiar tunes, with words that could teach the gospel truths even to people who couldn't read or write. His life was a frenzy of activity that didn't slow down even when church leaders threatened to have him arrested and killed.

Luther was a bridge between God and people who didn't know God yet. Through him, God was at work blessing the world. Through Luther and his work, God changed my life nearly 500 years later. Maybe his work has blessed your life too.

If so, let me say this again: You have been blessed *so that* you can be a blessing to others.

Maybe

One of the outcomes of Luther's work was that a new church was born. But this wasn't his intention. And when it happened, he was very clear that he did NOT want the members of this new church to be called "Lutherans." He wanted this new church to be called the Evangelical church. (In fact, that's what the "Lutheran" church is actually called in Germany, Luther's homeland.) *Evangelical* comes from a Greek word that means "good news."

Luther was trying to say that this is who we are, as Christians. *We are evangelists, which simply means people with good news to share.* We are people who share the story of Jesus and the message of God's love with everyone. And we do this *humbly*, knowing that we didn't do anything to deserve the gift of God's love in the first place. We do this *respectfully*, knowing that everyone we are talking to is, whether they know it or not, deeply loved by God. God made them, after all! We do this *expectantly*, knowing that God often comes to meet us in the face of strangers and that, in those meetings, we are changed too. We do this *joyfully*, knowing that every time we share the story of God's love we experience it in a deeper way. And we do this *confidently*, knowing that Jesus is right there with us when we do it. He promised. (Read Matthew 28:18-20.)

If and when we warm a bench, it is because we just need a little breather. Or because we have met someone who is curious about this God we know, and wants to hear more.

"Come and sit next to me," you might say. "Let me tell you what I know."

Maybe you'll even invite her to the gathering, to share the Meal with you and meet your friends. Maybe you'll find yourself standing beside her, both of you confessing your brokenness and your need for God's forgiveness in your life. Maybe she will hear something that day, as the Word is spoken, that touches and changes her.

Maybe not.

But you'll keep doing what you do.

You are the church.

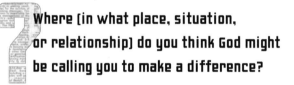 **Where (in what place, situation, or relationship) do you think God might be calling you to make a difference?**

Pray for

You will receive power when the Holy Spirit has come upon you; and you will be my witnesses in Jerusalem, in all Judea and Samaria, and to the ends of the earth.

Acts 1:8

4 | NO EXPERIENCE NECESSARY

God is on a mission and we have been created as partners. The Bible tells us all about this beginning with the book of Genesis. Why on earth then would God want *reading* the Bible to be complicated or sometimes hard to understand? It doesn't have to be. In fact, with a few basics in place, you can be reading the Bible—and getting something out of it—in no time.

Somewhere along the way I heard that the Bible has been the world's number-one best-selling book every single year since it was published. I can believe it. Nothing beats it. World sales top more than a million every year. If you did an online search of the word *Bible* you would get linked to more than 4.5 million sites in just 0.24 seconds! Obviously, a lot of us *own* Bibles. And a lot of us are *interested* in the Bible. But frankly, I'm not sure how much Bible *reading* is actually going on. Why is that?

Is it because the Bible is such a very old book that everybody assumes there's nothing worth reading in there anymore? Why would a 2,000-year-old book still matter? Or is it because people don't know where to begin and are simply overwhelmed at the prospect? Maybe it's because reading the Bible takes at least a little work and a little patience, and we are people who want what we want right now and are too overworked and too tired to put much effort into anything. I don't know.

But I do know that the Bible shows us a God who loves us, whose heart aches for us, and who is on a mission to make our world holy and whole. I know how badly we need a God like that. I also know that this is only the beginning. God calls each of us to be part of that mission. In fact, participating in God's mission in the world is what gives our lives meaning and purpose. The Bible shows us that too. But to see it, we've got to get that Bible off the shelf or out of storage, or maybe we just have to go buy a new one, and actually get into the Bible itself.

If you're looking to do that ... if you really want to hear what God is saying to you through the words of the Bible ... if you're hoping and praying that the God of the Bible can lead you into a life of meaning and purpose and real joy ... try the following.

Read the Bible like a Tom Clancy novel

I'm not kidding. That is the single best piece of advice I can give you when it comes to opening up the Bible. Read it like a good book, leisurely and thoughtfully. Because that, after all, is what the Bible is: at its core it's God's story.

However, when you open up this particular book, be prepared. No matter how much you read, you'll confront uncertainties. The biblical writers (and there are many) tried to be as clear as they could be. They wanted their readers to know exactly what they were trying to say about who God is and what God is up to in the world and what our role in it all is supposed to be. But that doesn't mean there won't be moments when you feel frustrated and confused. There will be references to customs you don't catch and cultural realities you don't know anything about. There will be places you don't recognize. There will be people you don't know and whose names you can't even pronounce. Especially toward the front of the Bible, there will be lists of rules and regulations so long, written for people so long ago, that you'll wonder for a moment what ever made you think reading this book would be a good idea in the first place.

Well, relax. And don't worry too much about all the things you don't understand or don't really care about. Just try reading the text like a Tom Clancy novel.

I love adventure books. In my opinion Clancy's are the best. You've got political intrigue, death-defying adventure, high-stakes espionage, heroic characters, diabolical villains, steamy romances, world-threatening crises, and breath-taking rescues in story after story. It's fascinating to read. This is what I do on my vacations. But I have had to overcome one small problem in order to enjoy these books. Clancy fills his novels with technical language and military slang that I know nothing about. Listen to this:

"Two new contacts, sir, designate Sierra Twenty and Twenty-one. Both appear to be submerged contacts. Sierra Twenty, bearing three-two-five, direct path and faint ... stand by ... okay, looks like a Han-class SSN, good cut on the fifty-Hertz line, plant noise also. Twenty-one, also submerged contact, at three-three-zero, starting to look like a Xia, sir."

"A boomer in a FleetEx?" the senior chief wondered.

—Tom Clancy, *Executive Orders*
(New York: G. P. Putnam's Sons, 1996), p. 373

Believe it or not, there are those who read Clancy novels because of his technical command of realistic detail. I have a friend like this. He's an engineer, of course, and a techno-geek. He loves the real-life lingo and the references to all the latest, greatest technological achievements. Me? I read these books in spite of that stuff. I read them because Clancy tells a good story and because I care about the characters. And somehow, I manage to get the point—even though the technical language goes right over my head.

It isn't much different for us when we sit down to read the Bible.

Like my friend, some of you will really enjoy the challenge of the technical details. You'll want to know more. Like, who wrote this stuff? And when did they write it? And where were they when they wrote it? And who was it written for? And what was the world like back then? And what did these words and stories mean in that context? In fact, for many years, these were the kinds of questions that most biblical scholarship focused on.

Most of us, however, are not biblical scholars or history buffs. And, when we sit down to read the stories in the Bible, a lot of the technical language is going to go right over our heads. Odds are, when you start reading you're going to be clueless about the historical context. You'll have no idea who most of the people are. And the geography, well, forget it. I myself don't know where a lot of countries are on the map today, much less thousands of years ago. But you know what? While knowing these things can be helpful and interesting, when it comes to reading the Bible and getting something out of it, they just aren't that important.

In fact, many scholars today have come to the conclusion that, as much as we'd like to know all the answers to those who-what-when-where kinds of questions, the Bible was written too long ago for us to ever know for sure. Even the experts today are learning how to read the Bible as a story.

The formal term for this method of reading the Bible is called a narrative approach. Scholars who read the Bible as story assume that the narrators of each story and every book were trying to make a point. We might not always know exactly who these narrators were. We do know there were many of them, including the original storytellers (those who circulated these stories orally from one generation to another), the writers (those who finally wrote these words down), and the editors (those who put all these stories together). We know that they all were part of the community of faith and that God was at work through them. And we know that they told these stories and wrote them down and put them all together for a reason. They were trying to tell us something. Scholars who use this narrative approach pay special attention to how a passage or story has been crafted in their effort to figure out what it is the narrator wants us to hear. They watch for the phrases, words, or images that get repeated along the way. They look for that turning point in the unfolding story, when the real drama happens. They listen to the Bible in their effort to get right to the point.

When you sit down with the Bible, don't be put off by the technical language or overly worried at what you don't get. Read it for what it is. Read it because you care about the characters (with whom, you will discover, you have a lot in common). Read it. Then ask yourself what the point of it all is. Read it because, with apologies to Mr. Clancy, it is the most exciting story ever told.

Know the basics

Now, once you're all settled to read this good book, it will help to know a few of the basics.

Start with knowing how to find your way around the Bible. First, every Bible is divided into two main sections: the Old Testament and the New Testament. (Some Bibles also include an Apocrypha, a collection of ancient writings considered valuable and worthwhile by Christians but that didn't make it into the official list of writings accepted by all Christians. The disputed books are generally placed in a separate section, usually bound between the Old and New Testaments.)

Second, the Old and New Testaments are both divided into books. Each book is divided into chapters. And within each chapter are numbered verses. The chapters and verses are numbered exactly the same in every version of the Bible, universally, in every language.

Being able to find your way around the Bible is important. It's also helpful to know a little about each of two main sections of the Bible.

The Old Testament

This part of the Bible tells the story of a God who is madly in love with the world. God created it! And God loves it. And, even though people keep trying to mess it up, God stays faithful to it. In fact, over and over again, God invites people to be partners in making things right. In the Old Testament, we learn about a very special relationship God formed with an ancient tribe, which eventually became known as the Israelites. The Israelites were chosen by God to be the ones through whom the whole world would be brought back to God. "I will bless you," God told Abraham and Sarah (patriarch and matriarch of the tribe), "so that you will be a blessing" (Genesis 12:2b). All this happened centuries before Jesus was born.

The Old Testament tells the story of these ancient people, and the way God has been at work in and through them, for the sake of the whole world. It was originally written in their language, Hebrew. Many different authors contributed to the books of the Old Testament, each attempting to capture the ancient oral traditions and stories in writing. This took time. In fact, some scholars suggest that more than a thousand years passed between the time the earliest and the latest passages were written down. It is hard to pinpoint exactly when the final form of the Old Testament was established, but it most likely happened before the year 200 B.C. (about 200 years before Jesus was born).

As you can imagine, the thousand-year history of an ancient people is a colorful one. There are wars and famines. There are scoundrels and saviors, tyrants and thieves, nomads and farmers. There is slavery and deliverance. Babies are born and kings are made and friends are betrayed. There is no short-age of adventure.

It is important and helpful, however, as you read the Old Testament to pay attention to the kind of writing you are dealing with in each case. The story gets told using many different forms and many different types of literature. There are historical accounts and wise sayings, prayers and poems and songs and fables. There are even a few long lists of rules and regulations, commandments and laws that helped these long-ago people live together peacefully, in good health. Honor the form. It wouldn't be right to read a poem as history, or to turn a rule that was made up for a particular situation into a hard-and-fast law for all time. The main thing to understand is that the stories of the Old Testament reveal a God who is passionate about the world. God is faithful to us, no matter how stubborn or stupid we are. God never turns away from us. Over and over again, in the Old Testament, God promises that one day things will be different. In fact, God wants to partner with us to make it different.

The New Testament

The New Testament continues the story of God's mission in this world. Here we meet Jesus, in whom we have the clearest picture of who God is and what God is up to. Jesus came announcing that the kingdom of God was near. And in his ministry we get a glimpse of what that kingdom looks like. Jesus is the Savior, who has been sent for all the people of the world. This Messiah rescues us from darkness and death, and delivers us from our own worst impulses, and puts us back on the path of life. When Jesus appeared, God showed up! The New Testament tells Jesus' story and the story of the movement, later called Christianity, which his life, death, and resurrection sparked.

The New Testament was written in Greek, the predominant language of that time. It begins with four books, called Gospels, with each Gospel written by a different person. They all include stories from the life of Jesus. They describe miracles he performed, sermons he delivered, people he met, his death, and his resurrection. The four Gospel writers are known as Matthew, Mark, Luke, and John. Some of these writers were actually on the scene, eyewitnesses to the events that took place during the life of Jesus. Others experienced these events through the first-hand reports given to them by actual witnesses. Each writer describes these events from a unique perspective. The result is that some of the details of the story differ from book to book.

There is complete agreement among the four writers about the one most important thing: that Jesus of Nazareth is the long-awaited Messiah, the Son of God and the Savior of the world. This is the good news that each of the New Testament writers intends for us to read in their stories. They want us to hear good news for our lives in the story of Jesus Christ. In fact, *gospel* is an Old English word that means "good news."

Following the four Gospels is a collection of books that includes letters written by the leaders of the early Christian church. The biggest letter writer of all was a man named Paul.

Paul traveled around starting new churches and, as he moved, he would keep in touch with the friends he had made by writing letters to them. In his letters he would continue to teach them about Jesus. He also filled his letters with practical advice about how the Christian faith might direct one's family life, marriages, work life, church life, and so on. This advice was always given to real people, in real situations. Some of it may sound strange to us today and may not really make sense in our context. But the point of it all is that our faith is supposed to impact every single aspect of our lives.

You can find Paul's own story in the book of Acts (chapter 9). Here we learn that Paul started out thinking Christians and this Jesus fellow they worshiped were crazy. Dangerous even. He had made it his own personal mission to hunt down bands of new Christians and have them put to death. In fact, he was on his way to do just that in a town called Damascus when he ran into the risen Jesus. Well, actually, Jesus spoke to him out of a light so bright that it blinded him and knocked him right off his high horse. Literally. Jesus in effect asked him, "What in the world do you think you're doing?" And that was pretty much all Jesus had to say. Once Paul got up and his eyesight finally came back, he started singing a different tune. And he sang it well. No one ever did a better job of getting the word out about Jesus than Paul did. You'll see what I mean when you read the rest of Acts.

The book of Acts, together with the letters that follow it, describe what happened in the early church after the living

Jesus departed earth and was taken up into heaven. It is the story of how the Holy Spirit worked through a handful of believers in ancient Jerusalem to reach all around the entire world.

Use your imagination

Hello! Are you still there?

After getting all comfortable and settled in to read, if you started to fade as we began talking about the kinds of issues, characters, and stories that are in the Bible, then you are experiencing one of the biggest problems a lot of people have when they sit down to read the Bible. It is what I call the sleep problem: as soon as you start reading, all you want to do is sleep. I am convinced this is because people expect the Bible to be boring.

How silly.

The Bible is God's own book. And God is a lot of things. Boring is not one of them. Picture the first snowfall of the season, big fluffy flakes and bright sunshine, hats and mittens pulled out of mothballs, sleds brought down from the rafters, the blast of wet coldness that hits you like a snowball that has found its mark and wakes you up and makes you feel alive. Or picture an evening in a funeral home, relatives embracing, children racing through the legs of their suddenly tolerant elders, and smiles breaking out through tears. Still further, picture the universe, which of course you can't because it is so vast, so unknowable, and ever so full of silent promise. Consider how it teases us into faith in a Being bigger than ourselves. Who else could have stirred into existence something so amazingly complex as the universe? Who else could take away the sting of death? Who else could have dreamed up snow? These things, all of them and more, are God's doing. Boring?

I don't think so. Why would God's book be any different?

If you look up the word *Bible* in an encyclopedia, it most likely will tell you that the Bible is one of the most famous and important books ever written. Literature, art, and drama have been more influenced by the words of the Bible than any other written work. You can read the Bible in more languages than any other book ever published.

What the encyclopedia will not tell you is that the Bible has changed people's lives. It is, today, changing the lives of some of the most important and powerful people in the world and of people you might walk right by and not notice. The Bible is changing my life, and maybe it is changing yours too.

Through the stories it tells, the Bible introduces you to a God who is loving and powerful and alive. You see God in action, parting the Red Sea (Exodus 14) and raising the dead to life (John 11:17-44). You hear the very voice of God, proclaiming liberty to the captives and comfort to the sick and hope to the brokenhearted (Isaiah 42:1-9; Luke 4:16-21). How could you meet this living God without being changed?

Just in case it wasn't enough to meet the almighty God in these stories, however, the Bible gives you a bonus. Through its stories you meet another very important person. You meet yourself. I know I have.

I've clearly seen myself in the mistake-making Peter (Luke 22:54-62) and the running-for-his-life Elijah (1 Kings 19:1-18) and the angry-as-hell Martha (Luke 10:38-42). I've seen myself in the woman at the well (John 4:1-42) surprised, embarrassed, and out of options. I've also seen myself embraced and forgiven and given a second chance, like poor doubting Thomas (John 20:19-29). The stories of the Bible are not just about a bunch of people long ago dead. They are about me and about my life. They are about you.

When you sit down to read the Bible, expect the best. Expect to be moved to tears, filled with hope, or caught off guard by laughter. Expect to be surprised and challenged and inspired and encouraged and changed. Expect to hear a living God speak to you about the issues and concerns and fears and needs in your life.

Of course, reading the Bible is not the only way we can hear God's voice. We can hear God *speak* to us in a sermon or during worship when we are told that our sins are forgiven. We can hear God *speak* to us in the midst of our troubles when a Christian friend assures us that God loves us and holds us close. The word of God, in fact, is much bigger than the Bible. *The word of God is Jesus Christ* (John 1:1,14). The word of God is living and at work in the world right now and would survive even if all the Bibles in the world disappeared. God's word could never be confined to the words of a sermon or to the words on any page (not even the Bible's). However, the Bible is one very important way that God speaks to us today. The Bible is God's *written* word and, so, it is the authority we turn to in questions of faith and daily life. And when we read it, we expect something to happen! We expect to be challenged and changed. We expect to hear God's voice.

The Bible is one very important way that God speaks to us today.

Each time you get ready to spend time reading your Bible, wait just a minute before you open it. In that moment ask God to show you something you really need to see. If you open the Bible, then, with a few basics under your belt and your imagination fired up and raring to go, I guarantee you won't find yourself falling asleep.

Start somewhere

Imagination ready, basics under your belt, ready for a good story ... now what? Well, just dive in. But, then again, where? Some people think you've got to start at the beginning of the Bible, with the book of Genesis. You don't. In fact, I usually recommend starting in the middle of the Bible with the book of Luke. Why? Luke tells us the story of Jesus. Knowing that story will help you make sense of all the rest of it. But mostly I just want to encourage you to read whatever interests you.

If you are intrigued by people and want to get a sense for how real God's people are (and how real God is to them), start by reading the book of Psalms. Every imaginable human condition and every conceivable emotion is represented there.

Psalm 4:1 demands: "Answer me when I call, O God of my right!" Psalm 40:1 gives thanks: "I waited patiently for the Lord; he inclined to me and heard my cry. He drew me up from the desolate pit." Psalm 60:1 complains: "O God, you have rejected us, broken our defenses; you have been angry; now restore us!" Psalm 84:4 sings for joy: "Happy are those who live in your house, ever singing your praise!" Read these psalms and you'll know there is nothing you could say to God that God hasn't already heard before. It'll free you up to be more honest with God than you have ever been.

If you want something serious to chew on, turn to Paul's Letter to the Romans. Paul was a scholar and wrote like one too. He wrote this particular letter to the Christians in Rome as a way of introducing himself and his faith to them before he dropped by for a visit. Unlike all of the other letters Paul wrote, which dealt with particular issues bothering the people he was writing to, Paul dwells on what he believed. It may take a while for you to figure out what he's saying in places. I still expect to be uncovering its meaning forty years from now. However, his main point is summed up in the first chapter: "I am not ashamed of the gospel. It is the power of God for salvation to everyone who has faith" (Romans 1:16). In other words, God loved us enough to send Jesus to save us. All of us. Hold on to that message as you read through the rest of his letter, and even the most confusing passages will be clearer.

And if you're a free spirit, just open up your Bible at random each day and discover what God might have to say to you through the passage that catches your eye. If you need a bit more structure read from a passage that has been cited in this chapter or start with a daily Bible reading plan. There are some offered on-line. Another idea would be to read a book at a time. How about the whole New Testament from start to finish? Or, go ahead, start at the beginning and work your way through to the end.

But start. Somewhere.

Find a study method that works for you

Just like there is no right place to start in your reading of the Bible, there is no one way to go about your reading, either. People use all kinds of methods to help them read and study the Bible. Some people find it helpful to keep a journal of their thoughts, prayers, and questions as they read. Others use a marker to highlight or a pen to underline passages and sections in the Bible that are especially meaningful to them. I've developed my own system using symbols next to passages to help me in my study. This way I can remember why I highlighted something, and it also helps me commit to memory more of what I've read. Here are some of the symbols I use:

☺	Made me laugh!
->	I really need to remember this.
!	This is a surprise!
???	What in the world does that mean?

Try it yourself. Come up with your own symbols or find some other method of Bible reading and study that works for you.

Get help

If at this point you begin to feel like reading the Bible is getting too complicated, get some help. In most bookstores where Bibles are sold you can find a variety of resources to help you learn to get around in the Bible and get something out of it.

One of the first decisions you'll have to make is which version of the Bible you want to read. Unless you are able to read ancient Hebrew or Greek, you will read from a translation. Scholars who are experts in ancient languages and cultures have worked on these translations drawing from the original Greek and Hebrew texts.

My preference is for a translation that's been written in contemporary English but that sticks closely to the original source language. The New Revised Standard Version (NRSV), the New International Version (NIV), the Contemporary English Version (CEV), and the New Living Translation (NLT) are more recent translations that sound more or less like everyday English but try faithfully to represent what the original authors wrote. They will even give you the literal Greek or Hebrew translation where they have chosen another way to say it.

Once you choose a version of the Bible, you'll want to decide what "extras" (if any) you want with it. You can buy an inexpensive paperback Bible without any bells or whistles or a hard-cover edition with more features. Some Bibles have a thumb index, listing the name of each book and making it easier to find the passage you are looking for. A Bible identified as either a learning or study Bible offers things like maps, charts, and time lines. Such Bibles also include helpful information about each book and even each story, making it easier to understand the context of what you are reading. There are study Bibles for every group imaginable—women, men, couples, teens, children, busy people, and so on—that feature commentary and reflections of special interest to the people in that category. There are also Bible dictionaries and commentaries available for a more serious and in-depth understanding of the historical context and contemporary meaning of every biblical passage. The choice you make will be an entirely personal one based on your price range and own special needs. There are tremendous resources available today to make Bible reading easier and more interesting (see "For Further Reading and Study," page 112). You can actually have fun choosing the resources that are best for you.

Personally, though, I have always found that as I struggle to read and understand the Bible the best source of help can be found in the face of a friend. Or two. There is no better way to really get something out of the Bible than to talk it over with others. Find a partner, if you can, or a small group of friends. Study the Bible together. Many congregations have Bible studies like No Experience Necessary (a related series of Bible study resources) that are open to newcomers and those well versed in

Bible study. Visit a few study groups and find one that's right for you. Or invite some people you know to start up a Bible study of your own. Oh, they might look at you funny the first time you suggest it. But my guess is, they are just as curious and just as much in need of God's good news as you are.

Where (in what place, situation, or relationship) do you think God might be calling you to make a difference?

Pray for

Hear, O Israel: The Lord is our God, the Lord alone. You shall love the Lord your God with all your heart, and with all your soul, and with all your might. Keep these words that I am commanding you today in your heart. Recite them to your children and talk about them when you are at home and when you are away, when you lie down and when you rise.

Deuteronomy 6:4-7

5 | EXPECT GREAT THINGS

If we are really going to be God's partners in mission, we are going to need a clear vision for where God is leading, courage to follow, and hope to carry us along the way. These are the kinds of things God gives to us through a healthy prayer life.

I have always had a tendency toward high hopes. Even at the age of nine, when it was clear my body was destined to spread out, not sprout up. As a child I never had a nickname but if I had it surely wouldn't have been "Cher" for, unlike Cher, it was clear my body was not to reach gracefully skyward.

Remember when Cher was on *The Sonny and Cher Show*? God help me, I wanted to be like Cher. She was strong, independent, and smart. And every time she flung that long, black hair over her shoulder, I felt my own confidence surge. "I can do anything!" her voice echoed in my head. "The world is mine!" Yes, it's true, I was young and hopelessly naive at the time but it was a time when girls dreamed dreams.

"When I grow up," I asked my dad one day, "can I be the president?"

"Honey," Dad said, "you can be anything you want to be."

Sonny, however, didn't inspire me. The only time I thought he really mattered was when the two sang their signature song together, the all-time ode to confidence "I Got You Babe."

No matter what else I might need but don't have, I got you babe and life is good. Dreams come true. Oh, what an era it was! Martin Luther King Jr. had a dream. Neil Armstrong must have had one too when he planted the U.S. flag on the moon. And then there was Evel Knievel, who dreamt up death-defying motorcycle jumps. There was nothing he couldn't jump over.

I miss those days. We still believed that anything was possible. Since then, we have shared disappointments and endured tragedy.

Today, Sonny's widow does her best to carry on where Sonny left off. Cher is in the middle of a decade-long good-bye. And it's been a very long time since I heard any public leader share a dream compelling enough to believe it. Time has indeed brought change, even a shift in our social paradigms.

Recent surveys show that most people today expect Social Security to be broke by the time they reach retirement age. Statistically, we expect fifty-one percent of U.S. marriages to fail. We expect half of our sons from African-American families to end up dead or in jail before they are thirty. We still expect our daughters to make less money and have fewer options than their brothers. At a time when technology can bring us closer, we are more aware of our global neighbors, many of whom distrust and dislike us. And we expect to distrust and dislike them. We expect too many children around the world to go to bed hungry every night. We elect our public officials based largely on the promises they make, but we don't really expect those promises to be kept. This generation is the first in American history to expect a lower standard of living than their parents enjoyed. In spite of the fact that the U.S. economy is stronger and more stable than any in the world, the savings rate in this nation is still ten percent lower than it is in most other industrialized countries. Why? Well, is it possible that people only save for a future they really believe they'll have? Is it possible that we are people united, not by our dreams, but by our lack of them?

Even those of us with a tendency toward high hopes find ourselves feeling cynical and scared. A whole new political and economic system appears to be emerging that is *dependent* on our fears. Politicians in their scramble to get votes speak of the dangers we face and try to convince us they will keep us safer than their opponents. And to keep ourselves safe we're drawn to the likes of an increasingly popular massive civilian vehicle (you can't really call it a car or even a truck) that costs $50,000 and up, a vehicle initially designed for the battlefield. It's hard to imagine a better or a safer or a more peaceful world, even for God's partners in mission.

But we are not the first of God's partners to feel like this. A long time ago, in a book filled with wise sayings, these words made their way into the Bible: "Where there is no prophecy, the people cast off restraint" (Proverbs 29:18). Another way to put it is: Without a *vision,* the people perish. In other words, when we stop seeing what God wants to show us and hearing the things God has to say to us, trouble is sure to follow.

If we really are going to be God's partners in this world, we need a clear vision of where God is leading us, courage to follow, and hope to carry us along the way. That has been true in every age. It's true today. This is something God offers to us through a healthy prayer life.

Learn to listen

Joe and his family had worshiped pretty regularly for a couple of years when I asked to meet with him. Every year I would make a point to visit three or four individuals in the congregations I served to talk with them about their giving. This was Joe's year. My goal was to invite Joe to tithe, to take a leap of faith in his giving and give away ten percent of his income. A bold request, yet one that could have profound effect on his spiritual life. I had seen that happen in my own spiritual growth. When you tithe, you partner with God in a very serious way to make a difference in the world. You learn to trust God's promise to give you everything you need as you do. It's awesome. Anyway, that was my agenda that night. Joe, however, had something else on his mind.

We went into the family room and sat down. I smiled. He looked agitated. I said I was glad he agreed to meet with me. "I'm glad you came," he said. "I've been wanting to talk to you."

For the next hour or so, Joe told me about his life, about how hard he had worked to get where he was. He told me about how he had everything he ever thought he wanted—a great wife, great kids, a great house, and a great job. Everything was great, he said. Great. Except for one thing. He felt like there was a big hole right in the middle of it all. He felt empty. He said he had thought about changing jobs, moving to another state, taking his family and starting over somewhere, doing something radically different to try to fill up the emptiness.

"I've prayed about this," he said. And he said it in a way that made me believe him. "But I don't hear God answer. *I* don't hear anything." He actually looked a little desperate.

Joe confessed that he was starting to think God didn't exist and, if God was there, he didn't think God was paying much attention. Joe talked and talked, which was good because I wasn't quite sure what to say.

"Do you pray?" he asked suddenly.

"Yes," I said.

"Do you hear God answer you?"

"Yes," I said gently. I knew this would hurt him. "Yes, I do."

This made Joe look really sad. No, I take that back. It made him look sad ... and *angry*.

"Well, how do you know it's God?" he asked sharply. "How do you know you're not just hearing what you want to hear?"

I knew I didn't have a lot of leeway with Joe that night. I had to be honest and clear.

"Joe," I said, "how much time have you ever spent reading the Bible?"

"Not a lot. Why?"

"The Bible is one way God speaks to us. It isn't the only way. But it is where God's word is written down. *When you read the Bible you begin to learn what God's voice sounds like.* If you're trying to pray without truly reading the Bible, you'll find it hard to listen. You don't have any practice listening."

Like Joe, we too must realize that a healthy prayer life begins with learning to listen. And that begins when we read the Bible. That's where we learn what God's voice sounds like. We learn about the kinds of things that are important to God. We learn about how God gets things done. We learn about who God is. We learn *God always hears us when we pray.* Reading the Bible makes it easier for us to hear God. Through reading the Bible, we see God has a vision. More than anything we could have dreamed of.

Dare to speak

You have read the text and you've spent time listening. Now comes prayer. The Bible tells us that there is no more powerful thing a person can do than pray. In prayer, God opens our minds to imagine new possibilities and gives us courage to do what seems impossible. God helps us hang in there when we find ourselves down on our knees in despair because everything seems so hopeless. Praying is what Daniel was doing that night in the lions' den. And no, the lions didn't eat him (read Daniel 6:1-28). It's what Paul and Silas were doing as they sat in a prison cell; God answered them with an earthquake that literally broke open their jail and set them free (read Acts 16:11-40). It's what Jesus did before he chose his disciples, when faced with temptation, when tired and in need of renewed strength, and when surrounded on all sides by enemies. I guess you could say Jesus prayed pretty much all the time. It's what he was doing the night before he saved the world (read Luke 22:39-46). Prayer begins with learning to listen. But it also includes daring to speak.

Now, it is interesting and important to note that the Bible hardly ever tells us what God's people were saying as they prayed. Although Jesus gave the disciples The Lord's Prayer (read Luke 11:1-4) when they asked for help learning how to pray, he did not tell them this was the only way to pray. In fact, nowhere in the Bible is there some prescribed formula we're supposed to follow, no template we're expected to pull up each time we pray. There are no right words assigned to the task.

This means, of course, that there is no wrong way either. And don't let anyone tell you otherwise. The truth is, I think, no two people pray the same.

I pray best in the shower. Okay, I know that may be a bit too personal for some people, but listen: There is something incredible about the water rushing over me, as clean and renewing as a baptismal rain. It makes me feel glad to think that I'm the child of a God who is so very eager to hand out second chances, who calls people like me into partnership and into a purposeful life.

The car is another place I have found myself talking to God. I often do this out loud, figuring my fellow commuters will think I'm singing along with the radio.

When I pray usually I use very ordinary language. It isn't that I see God as a friend exactly, at least not all the time. I am too often completely mystified by something God has done or astonished by something that has happened for which I can find no other explanation than God. Sometimes I am really mad at God, and at those moments I don't even want God to be my friend. I use ordinary language mostly because that is the only language I own. My words often come spontaneously and are driven by some hurting or happy or haunted place within me. I just talk.

Formal prayers can be useful too. As a rule, though, I rely on them only when I can't find any words of my own to use. I dread those times. But I am thankful for those prayers. Praying the Hail Mary got me through a blinding snowstorm one scary night on my way home from college one Christmas break. And I can always somehow manage to choke out the Lord's Prayer at a funeral even when all other words have failed me.

There really is no right or wrong way to pray. In fact, the only mistake you could make would be to expect nothing to happen when you do pray.

Expect great things

In my own life, if I'm not careful, my prayer life can be reduced to things like, "Please, God, just help me get through this day!" Or, as I'm pulling up to a family get-together, "Please help us all get out of this alive!" Or simply, faced with one crisis or another, "Oh, God!"

I know I'm not alone in this. So many people pray these kinds of "prayers," there is actually a term used to describe them. They're called "foxhole prayers." Prayers of desperation shouted at the universe in the hopes that someone, somewhere will hear. Personally, I have never been in a foxhole. So I prefer to call these

God promises great things when we pray.

"parking lot prayers." As in: "%@&!#* it, God, I'm late! I don't have all day to find a parking space!"

However, this is not a prayer life and these are not really prayers. They are wishes.

The difference between praying and wishing is this: Praying depends on God. Wishing depends on luck; and luck is unreliable. Just ask the guy who won $16.2 million in the Pennsylvania lottery a few years back. Since then, if I have the story right, he was arrested for assault, his sixth wife left him, and his brother was convicted of trying to kill him. Think twice about putting your faith in luck.

God, on the other hand, promises great things when we pray. If the Bible tells us anything about prayer, it is this: Don't waste it! Pray for something worthy of the powerful, almighty, and ever-living God. Be clear. Be specific. Be outrageous. And expect something amazing to happen when you do it.

The apostle Paul had great expectations. He's famous for the outlandish things he expected from God. He asked for things that no one in his day had dreamt about. He asked for things worthy of a great and mighty God, a God whose power at work in us can do far more than we dare ask or imagine (read Ephesians 3:20-21). Sustained by his confidence in a God who can do wondrous things for us and *through* us, for the sake of the world, Paul faithfully and courageously faced disappointment, rejection, imprisonment, loneliness, and betrayal. He expected God to do great things.

When we listen, we can expect God to speak. And when we speak, we can expect God to listen.

In all the stories that are told about him, Jesus is never caught ignoring anyone who called upon him for help. Oh, he might have argued with them a little about whether or not they really needed what they thought they did. But he never just ignored people. It didn't matter how tired or worn out he was, or how distracted or distressed. At one point, in fact, Jesus was especially distressed and tried to leave the crowds. He had just been told that King Herod had murdered his cousin John. He went away to some place where he could be alone to pray and, I would guess, to pull himself together. But a crowd of people followed him, wanting him to teach and heal them. When Jesus saw them, he felt sorry for them. Instead of coping with his grief in private, he spent the whole day ministering to them (read Matthew 14:13-21). Jesus was always there when he was needed. In fact, he made this promise: "Everyone who asks receives, and everyone who searches finds, and for everyone who knocks, the door will be opened" (Luke 11:10).

So, what are you asking for these days? Is it a worthy search? Is it worthy of the mission to which God has called you? Is it earth-moving, life-changing, peace-making, hunger-ending, and kingdom-bringing enough? Is it so big that it could only ever actually happen if God was involved? Does it take your breath away?

If so, that is a prayer worth praying.

Be patient

Now God, being God, doesn't always answer on our timetable. In almost the same breath, Jesus told his listeners to be patient and not to give up just because things do not appear to be happening. Jesus said be persistent in prayer (read Luke 8:5-10). Hang in there while God goes to work. God *will* go to work. Even if we manage to go into prayer confidently, expecting an answer, waiting is another story.

We don't like to wait for anything. Take a look at our eating habits. One of today's fastest growing markets in the food industry seems to be prepared foods. A lot of us have gotten used to eating our salads out of a bag, dressing and croutons and all. BBQ now comes in a bucket in the refrigerated section of your local grocery store. And that chicken breast at the meat counter? Well, some chef somewhere has already magically turned it into chicken kiev. Just heat and eat. We are not a patient people. We know what we want and we want it now. And, even if we can't afford it, we won't wait longer than it takes to pull out a credit card to have it.

We are impatient people, even in the best of times.

But do you know what it's like to be at that point, where everything looks hopeless? Where God seems to live across some silent wasteland? Where you can't think of a single reason not to quit? I do. I have felt that way at work and I have felt that way at home. I have felt that way listening to Christians argue with each other about who should be welcomed at the Lord's Table, and who we can pray with, and who we'll allow to serve as pastors. I have felt that way listening to the news on the radio. I have found myself wondering what is taking God so long.

And, then, I remember Jairus. Luke 8:40-56 tells us that Jairus was a leader in his community, a man used to being in control and doing things his own way. But when we meet him he is desperate. He is so desperate that he is willing to do things God's way. You see his little daughter is sick. In fact, she's dying.

Jairus fought his way through the crowd to get to Jesus. He repeatedly begged Jesus, the story says, to come with him and do something to heal his daughter. And Jesus right away went with him. But as they were going, a large crowd followed Jesus and pressed in on him, blocking his way, making demands, and slowing him down. The story tells us that one woman, who had been hemorrhaging for twelve years, touched the edge of his cloak until she was healed. That delayed things even more.

It's not until verse 49 that we finally get back to Jairus. Desperate Jairus. It must have felt to him like decades had gone by—even eons. And then only to have some people from his neighborhood come and tell him to forget it all and to go home. It's too late. His daughter was dead.

If ever there was a moment to call it a day, to throw in the towel, to go home and cry yourself silly, this was it. Instead Jesus replied, "Do not fear. Only believe" (Luke 8:50).

Even when Jairus was ready to give up, Jesus didn't. When Jesus arrived at Jairus's home, he found the girl and healed her. She got up and had breakfast. Jairus, I imagine, embraced his daughter and felt the warmth of life in her and cried thankful tears. I'd be willing to bet he vowed never again to expect too little or give up too soon.

Whatever it is you are praying about these days, don't give up. No matter how hopeless, how desperate, or how alone you feel, hang in there. God will bless all your struggling, all the giving, all the forgiving, all the sacrificing, all the truth-telling, all the temptation-resisting, all the hard-road-taking. God will not leave you, ignore you, or disappoint you. God hears you. God will answer. Count on it.

Prepare to go to work

Trusting that God hears us, and also answers our prayers, however, is not the end of the story. The Irish have a saying: If you're going to pray for potatoes, you'd better pray with a hoe in your hand. And here's the truth: The more you get to know God through the kind of prayer life that begins with the Bible, the more you will discover a God who wants to put you to work doing something that really matters with your life.

I remember the day that Chicago's Cardinal Joseph Bernardin announced his cancer was terminal. He had been praying for healing and worked hard for it, doing everything his doctors told him to do. His reward, it seemed, was a clean bill of health in mid-August 1996. But by September 1, the doctors reversed their evaluation. Bernardin was told he had less than a year to live. In the flurry of media moments that followed, the cardinal acknowledged there would be some dark and difficult days ahead. He never minimized the anxiety and pain of the condition that he shared with so many others. But he assured everyone that he was at peace. He even called his cancer a special gift from God and believed his illness would give him a unique opportunity to teach and to lead. The way the cardinal faced his death taught many of us more about life than anything else he had ever done.

Hearing that his cancer was back surely was not the answer to prayer that Cardinal Bernardin had hoped to hear. But realizing the impact he had on the lives of so many the cardinal would say that he *did* get an answer. His answer was an invitation to be a part of God's mission to bless the world and a *promise* that his life would mean something.

When we meet God in prayer, we are able to see things we would never have seen on our own. We find courage to do things we would not otherwise have been able to do.

This takes me back to my friend Joe. He got up one morning after my visit and opened up his Bible to the book of Genesis, chapter 1, verse 1. And he began to read. He did this every morning for a year until he had read through the entire Bible. When he was done he went back to the book of Genesis and started all over again. He's been doing this for three or four years now. And apparently he's learned how to listen. You can see it in his actions. Not only has he started giving away a portion of his income, he's head of the stewardship team in that congregation, and in that role he encourages others to follow his lead. He teaches confirmation to a bunch of seventh and eighth graders on Monday nights. And he's joined the preaching team. He's told the whole congregation about that empty hole at the center of his life and how being a part of what God is up to was the only thing that could ever really fill it.

A life of prayer that grows out of an encounter with the Bible will lead to a life of action. A life of action lived in response to God's call to partnership depends on prayer.

Pray. Act. Pray.
Repeat.
It is as simple—and as demanding—as that.

Where [in what place, situation, or relationship] do you think God might be calling you to make a difference?

Pray for

Rejoice always, pray without ceasing, give thanks in all circumstances; for this is the will of God in Christ Jesus for you.

1 Thessalonians 5:16-18

6 | THE LIVER INCIDENT

Right up there with sharing the story of God's love is sharing our stuff. We have been blessed to be a blessing. Jesus talked about this issue more than any other. It must be pretty important.

You've heard of all the great showdowns, moments in history when someone scores a victory over another after a match-up of some sort.

But you haven't heard of the liver incident. Until now.

I was, I think, about five.

And I hated liver. This was not just a mild dislike. This was an "I'm gagging and I think I'm going to die" kind of dislike. This was a "There is no way in the world you can make me eat this, not even if you make me sit at this kitchen table until the rest of my class is graduating from high school" kind of dislike. And the worst thing was: Mom knew it. I know she did.

Here's what I recall. We were planning to go to my grandma's house after dinner. This venture out, I suspect, was meant to motivate me to do the unthinkable: eat that now cold piece of liver sitting there on my plate. But there was just no way under the sun that was going to happen. Everyone else had finished before I did. I was determined to hold out. I was not about to eat that thing! Mom thought differently. "Now clean your plate, young lady, and be sure to finish all that good liver," Mom said as she left the table to get ready to leave.

As soon as she left the room, I picked up my plate and scraped that disgusting piece of meat right into the garbage can and out of my life forever. That is until she found it there.

"That was quick," she said on her return to the room poised to challenge what I had just done. "Did you eat it all?" "Yes, Mom." I lied. "Every last bite."

Needless to say, I didn't get to Grandma's house that night and I did get a lecture. I bet you've heard it too. It went something like this: "You should be thankful you have food on your plate at all, young lady. Children are starving in...." And then she named a location. My thought back then was: "Well, go ahead and send it to them. They won't like it either!" But now I know my mom was right. I was blessed to have food on my plate. Even liver.

More than enough

I believe that God too wants us to see how really blessed we are. God's word tells us so.

Abraham and Sarah were two people for whom God spelled this out. In Genesis 12, God makes it clear. "Abraham," God says in so many words, "I am going to bless you beyond your wildest imagination. You're going to have everything you could ever need. And I am going to do this *so that, through you, the whole world will be blessed.*" Then, in the very next chapter, God takes Abraham out on a walk (read Genesis 13:14-17).

"Rise up," God tells him, "walk through the length and the breadth of the land, for I will give it to you" (Genesis 13:17). In other words, "Abraham, everything you see in every direction for as *far* as you can see is yours. Go ahead. Walk the land. Walk every square inch of it! And as you walk remember it is I who gave it to you."

Just like Abraham, it is God's intention that we too *walk the land* that God has given to us, every square inch of it. We too need to look at the blessings God has showered upon us and on our lives, our families, our congregations, and our nation. I invite you to look at the blessings God has given to you. Take stock of all of what God has provided. See, just see, if you can even take it all in. Let yourself be amazed.

Our culture, of course, doesn't make it very easy for us to be grateful. Our whole economy depends on each of us being forever dissatisfied with what we do not have. For instance, my favorite hamburger joint beckons me through its advertising to come satisfy that craving. But really what they want is for me to crave more. We all know that. Nobody who sells stuff for a living really wants that hunger for more to ever go away.

Yet God's people have resisted the constant need for more. Throughout the ages, God's faithful have walked the land and given thanks for all they had. They have done this even when from the world's perspective it didn't look like they had very much.

Suffering persecution, without friends, and fearing for his life, the apostle Paul wrote, "Give thanks in all circumstances; for this is the will of God in Jesus Christ" (1 Thessalonians 5:18). Notice that Paul doesn't qualify his statement. He doesn't say be thankful when everything is going great and the sun is shining and your boss knows how lucky she is. Paul simply says be thankful. Always. Sometimes, of course, you have to look twice—or twenty times—to find something to be thankful for. But it's there.

God's people have been a thankful people too. As a young shepherd boy, not wealthy by any measure, living in the kind of constant danger that comes from working alone in the wilderness, David sang, "My cup overflows" (Psalm 23:5). It's too bad everybody thinks that psalm is only for funerals. The psalm is really talking about how great life is when God is in it. It looks us right in the eye and shouts, "Look at what you have, friend. And see how rich you are!"

There is a corny little game I like to play with my friends. We imagine that we are stranded on a desert island with no hope of rescue. And then we list the five material things (excluding people and pets) that we would most like to have with us. You know what's weird? This isn't hard to do. We know what we have that really matters to us. What would make your list? A favorite musical instrument? A hand-me-down tool? A special book? Your photo albums? A well-used recliner? Your feather pillow?

We actually need very few material things. And we have been given so very much more than that.

Growing up

I don't know why it is but in some ways it is almost easier for us to acknowledge the spiritual blessings God gives us. We are showered with God's forgiving and unconditional love. We are issued an undeserved and unexpected invitation to be a part of what God is up to in the world. These are gifts and we know it. We know there is nothing we could ever do to earn these things.

So why would we think we have earned the material things we have? Why would we for a moment think, "I know God's love here on earth and my ticket to heaven is a gift I don't deserve, and I am thankful beyond words for it ... but, doggone it, I DESERVE that plasma TV!"?

The truth of this life is that every single thing we have— spiritual and material—is a gift from God. God blesses us with these things because God wants our lives to be full and rich and happy.

But God also knows that true happiness comes when with overflowing hearts we give these things away. In fact, Jesus said that if we try to keep these things to ourselves ... we would die. "Those who want to save their life will lose it," he said. "And those who lose their life for my sake will save it" (Luke 9:24). This is a puzzle that only gets solved when we experience what happens when we actually do what Jesus calls us to do. Or when we experience what happens when we don't.

You have seen the shriveled soul of someone who has tried to hoard her wealth, haven't you? And you've seen the expansive, joyful spirit of people who generously and freely give away what they have.

It seemed ironic to me, when I was a young pastor, that the people who complained the most were invariably the ones who gave the least to the ministry of the congregation. Those who gave generously, tithing and beyond, were the ones who quietly led the way and cheerfully did whatever had to be done. They were the ones who could be counted on to pray for the ministry; the ones who faithfully supported the effort to seek the Spirit's direction, even if it meant moving into unfamiliar territory; the ones who firmly and gently held the leadership accountable for keeping the congregation on track in pursuing God's mission. These are the people I decided early on I wanted to be like when I grew up. I wanted to be like Aunt Ruth and Aunt Hazel and Aunt Gen, women whose lives spilled over to bless others and who blessed mine.

God told Abraham and Sarah that they would be blessed *so that* they could be a blessing to others. And that is true for us too. But it is also true that it is in blessing others that we are most deeply blessed. Real blessings come only when we give away what we have.

Start here

God is on a mission to bless the world and calls us through Christ to be a part of it. That means the Christian life is a generous life. Everything given to us is for the purpose of blessing others. We find real happiness as we fulfill that purpose, giving our stuff (and ourselves!) away.

And all of this begins right here ... at home.

It has been said that the primary characteristic of the early Christian community was their love for one another. They shared everything. Not one among them was in need. They left us their example to follow, and their words of encouragement. Read Hebrews 13. There you will find a random list of advice, admonitions if you will, on how to live the Christian life. Kind of an odd book in some ways, Hebrews is full of wonderful passages like this one. God wants us to start here: "to let mutual love continue" (verse 1).

A mom signed up to attend a parenting class her congregation was to offer. She was worried that she had been neglecting her two oldest children, both girls, because her attention was so focused on the needs of her youngest, a little boy who was born with a serious illness. The girls had grown up fast. Early on they had learned to share their mom's time with their younger brother. Nights were hard since the brother would often need his mom at his bedside. His cries would wake up everyone. But the girls were never scared. They had each other. They'd climb back into bed and whisper words of mutual encouragement. They knew their mom loved them. In that moment they also knew where their mom needed to be—with their little brother. That mom didn't need to worry. There was plenty of love in her house to go around.

That's how it should be. If any one of us has a problem, we all do. If any one of us has something to celebrate, we all do. That's what families ... friends ... neighborhoods ... and congregations are for.

An example. I thought I had graduated from seminary equipped to go teach people something. Actually, I was the one who was taught. I learned my first lesson on my very first day as a pastor at the hospital where I met with a family from the congregation. All were distraught over the just-pronounced death of a loved one. He had been fighting cancer for a long time. But the end, even if expected, is never easy. I struggled like the novice I was to find something, anything, to say. I left there with a promise to show up later at their house and hoped I'd have thought of what to say by then. When I got there they were kind enough to open the door and let me in. It was then that I was greeted by the smell of love. You didn't know it had a smell, did you? Well, it does. It's the smell of freshly baked bread. Pie. Hamburger casserole. Meatballs. All of it delivered to the house by those who knew how to share the love that they themselves had received.

This is where we should all begin. Right here. Having been so richly blessed, we should fill our homes and congregations and neighborhoods with love and generosity and joyfulness.

Let it flow

But, that "right here" is just a beginning if we are truly willing to listen to what the Bible has to say. The "right there" has to follow. We can't simply share "here" until we've shared "there," as well: "Do not neglect to show hospitality to strangers, for by doing that some have entertained angels without knowing it" (Hebrews 13:2).

Share with those who are on the outside, the Bible tells us. Strangers. Those who look and act and smell different than you and I do. Share with the poor. The sick. The faithless. The ugly, and yes, even the mean, because God cares for and loves us all. In fact, share the very *best* of what you have. (Isn't that what it means when we're told to share our homes?!) Do not stop sharing until the love God pours into you fills you up and then overflows spilling right out your front door and down your street and across the world.

> Do not stop sharing until the love God pours into you fills you up and then overflows.

A woman I know is shy in crowds to the point of painful humiliation. Yet somehow she has managed to welcome more people into her congregation than anyone else I know. I don't even know how she knows so many of them but she keeps inviting them. And they keep coming. She says it's easy. She loves her congregation. But I know it is because she loves people. She sees their hurt, their pain, their worry, and their need. And she knows there is something in the congregation that can help them.

Jesus shocked everybody when he said: "When you give a luncheon or a dinner, do not invite your friends or your brothers or your relatives or rich neighbors, in case they may invite you in return, and you would be repaid. But when you give a banquet, invite the poor, the crippled, the lame, and the blind. And you will be blessed, because they cannot repay you, for you will be repaid at the resurrection of the righteous" (Luke 14:12-14).

Most of us will never actually do this. But we could simply begin to see all people the way Jesus saw them: worthy of love and respect. We could share more. We could share a lot more. We could share our money, our time, and our skills. We could share our hearts and open up our homes. We could offer words of support and encouragement. We could share a smile. We could share a meal. We could simply share.

We've all learned from nutrition specialists that a "clean plate" isn't a practice we ought to perpetuate. So my kids are off the hook on that one. And I would never dream of cooking liver for dinner, much less expect it to be eaten. But I do ask my kids to tithe ten percent of their allowance each week, a practice they learned when they were small. They are learning how to share.

And they really are learning. Here's a story to illustrate. Several years ago I drove my then six-year-old son to day camp. On the way I realized I didn't have my wallet. That meant I didn't have the fifty cents he needed to buy a treat at the canteen. That's the best part of the day at summer camp! The part he looked forward to the most. He was distraught. Just before he completely lost it, I had an idea. "Hey, I bet we can scrounge up fifty cents in change right here in the car!" And we did. Ethan began frantically collecting change from between the seat cushions and under the floor mats. In fact, before the search was over he had uncovered almost a dollar. We continued our drive to camp happy and relieved. "You know," I said as we drove along, as much to myself as anyone, "I just thought of something. Some in the world have only fifty cents to feed an entire family for a whole day. And we simply have it lying around the floor of our car." Ethan didn't say anything. But when I looked over at him, big tears rolled down his cheeks.

You see, Mom was right, darn it. We are blessed. In more ways than we can count. We have more than enough of everything to go around. Ethan knows that.

We too know that when we answer the call to be a part of God's mission to bless the world it brings both meaning and purpose to our lives. This is, in fact, one way to sum up the purpose of our lives. We have been blessed to be a blessing. We have been given what we have in order to share it with others. And that includes our stuff.

Let it flow.

Where (in what place, situation, or relationship) do you think God might be calling you to make a difference?

Pray for

And God is able to provide you with every blessing in abundance, so that by always having enough of everything, you may share abundantly in every good work.

2 Corinthians 9:8

7 | THE TELLTALE TRIKE

We are not alone on this adventure. Being a part of God's mission in the world means being part of a community. Life together can be a challenge, but God makes it possible.

Many families have stories that are told around the table each Thanksgiving. These are the stories that have entered the family mythology and that help the family define itself. These stories usually begin with "Remember when...." Then everyone happily turns their attention to the teller, hoping this isn't "their" story but rolling their eyes good-naturedly when it is.

"Remember when Great-Grandma tipped the picnic bench over, sent her paper-plate flying, and lost her wig?!?" someone will say, conjuring up hysterical memories of our rather plump but usually decorous matriarch. And then, the story about our larger-than-life, always-right, never-lost-a-fight grandfather: "Remember when Grandpa went running through the neighborhood chasing Godfrey (a new puppy) with a rolled-up newspaper in his hand, yelling, 'God.... Come here, God!' and swearing he'd kill him?!?" And "Remember when...."

"Yes, yes! I remember," everyone says, even those too young to have been there for the event.

There is a little story sometimes told about me. The story of a telltale trike. My mother tells it to explain why I am the

way I am whenever somebody complains about me, which they occasionally do. Well, not "they." Usually my brother is the one complaining. The eighteen months that separate us have never been quite enough. "That's Kelly," my mom says when the crabby, stubborn, little demon inside of me is acting up again. "I remember when she was about two-and-a-half years old. She was outside on the sidewalk between our house and the neighbor's with her new, red tricycle. Suddenly I heard a terrible noise. I ran to the back door and there she was. Her tricycle was all tangled up and, apparently, she was having trouble getting it to work right. So, instead of coming in and asking for help ... instead of patiently working on the problem until it was solved ... she was just kicking the trike down the sidewalk." Everyone always laughs at this story because it isn't just a story about something that happened forty years ago. It's a story about now.

A holy MESS

As a little kid, I learned the finger rhyme: "Here is the church. Here is the steeple. Open the doors and see all the people." I taught that rhyme to my own children. It's cute. And it's fun to see small children get their fingers all tangled up trying to mimic their moms and dads. But the rhyme is wrong. In reality, you can't see people *inside* the church. Because together *we are the church,* a community of God's people. People like me. This explains why it is so often such a holy MESS.

Groucho Marx wrote, "I don't care to belong to any club that will have me as a member." I could say the same thing about the church. I know what's wrong with me, one deficit after another. (Just ask my brother. Or, better yet, take a second look at that mangled, tangled-up trike.) But the church let me in anyway.

Jesus got into trouble for not being choosy enough about who his friends were; he provided this example for the church. From the very beginning two thousand years ago, the church let anybody in—all sorts of people, even people who no respectable citizen would be caught dead with. Or alive, for that matter.

This means the church has always been made up of very ordinary, very flawed people. No wonder we fight with each other and make such a mess of things so often.

The church is people. And people are often insensitive to each other. Sometimes we are just plain mean. People can be selfish. People can be dumb. Jesus knew this better than anybody. He was so certain we would mess things up with each other that he gave very specific instructions about what to do when this happens. When you get into a disagreement with another member of the community, Jesus said, don't even bother coming to worship until you get it straightened out. Go make up. Forgive each other. Get over it (read Matthew 5:21-24).

> **Jesus addressed the issue of how to deal with community conflict because he knew it was inevitable.**

Jesus addressed the issue of how to deal with community conflict because he knew it was inevitable. You see, Jesus had to wrestle with conflict himself. He faced opposition from people outside of his band of followers. Did you know that he also faced opposition from within this group? For example, a big fight broke out when the mother of James and John, two of Jesus' disciples, tried to get them places of honor with Jesus. (To find out if she succeeded in doing this, read Matthew 20:20-28.) When some parents tried to bring their young children to Jesus to be blessed, his bone-headed disciples tried to chase them all away. Jesus was angry about this and told them so (read Mark 10:13-16). When Jesus explained to the disciples that he would have to die to fulfill his mission, Peter yelled at him (read Matthew 16:21-23; Mark 8:31-33). And one of Jesus' best friends turned him over to the authorities in an astounding act of betrayal that eventually led to Jesus' death (read John 13:21-30; John 18:1-8).

The little community that followed Jesus around was anything but idyllic. There was, in fact, a lot of fighting going on. Jesus' followers were just a bunch of very ordinary human beings. And wherever there are people, there is going to be trouble.

That is why Paul wrote so many letters. He wrote to the churches in places like Galatia and Corinth. Paul started all of these churches himself. He would come into a new town, get to know some locals, and settle down for a few years to teach people about Jesus. Once they seemed to have the hang of it, he would move on to another town and do the whole thing all over again. He would leave people in charge of each church and entrust them to carry on. But, inevitably, they would mess things up. They would start fighting about who should be the leader, how to worship, who should be allowed to join them, and what to believe. As soon as Paul found out about their fighting and disagreements, he would fire off a letter to try to straighten things out.

Paul was especially upset with the Christians in Galatia because they had messed up the very core of his teaching: that we are saved by grace and loved by God—not by anything we have done to earn or deserve it, but as a gift. For Paul, there was no compromising on this. "You foolish Galatians!" he wrote (Galatians 3:1), how could you get such a very important thing so wrong?

Paul wrote to the church in Corinth partly because they were constantly at each other's throats. In his letters, he pleaded with them to stop fighting: "Now I appeal to you, brothers and sisters, by the name of our Lord Jesus Christ, that all of you be in agreement and that there be no divisions among you, but that you be united in the same mind and the same purpose" (1 Corinthians 1:10). In fact, we have two letters from Paul to the people in Corinth. They had all sorts of problems!

Inconsistency, crabbiness, and disagreements in the church are nothing new. They have always been present in the church and, frankly, there is no reason to believe that, in this world, they will disappear.

It is easy to point out really big ways that the church has messed up. We could start and end with the Inquisition, when people in the Middle Ages were secretly put on trial and often tortured for disagreeing with the church's belief system. Or we could go on and add to that ignoble chapter in church history, the Crusades (a series of Christian military efforts to take over the Holy Land from the eleventh through thirteenth centuries), schisms or divisions within the church, indulgences (which were said to pardon the sins of those who bought them), persecution of scientists, misguided passion of missionaries, and the historical justification of slavery and the denigration of women. In fact, I meet a lot of people who use such a list to justify their conviction that "I'll never set foot inside another church. They're all just a bunch of hypocrites!"

But for most of us, our own personal stories are all we need to prove the point that the church is a mess. Those of us who hang in there week after week can tell about some congregation or some pastor or some "so-called" Christian letting us down, hurting and disappointing us, scaring us or pushing us further than we were ready and willing to go.

Here's one example from a woman who moved into a new home and started visiting a nearby congregation. One Sunday morning, after she had been visiting for several weeks, she mustered up the nerve to talk to the pastor. "I really like it here," she said. "The sermons are pretty good and the music is excellent. People seem friendly here." But when she told the pastor where she lived, he said, "Oh, you can't come here. You need to go to _____ on the other side of town. That's the church for your neighborhood." So she quit going to that church—or to any church. When I met her, this woman hadn't attended worship in more than eleven years. But she promised me that she would visit the congregation I was part of. She said she'd give it another try. She never did.

The truth is, the church is a mess. It always has been. From the beginning, the church has been full of people like me. I know, therefore, not to even bother asking myself, "Why do people in the church act that way?" The better question is, "With so many people like me in the church, how does the church survive?"

A HOLY mess

In fact, there is only one explanation for how the community of faith has survived all these years: It is an act of God. If I am the reason the church is such a mess, God is the reason the church is *holy*. Paul wrote to his friends in far-off Ephesus that the church is "built upon the foundation of the apostles and prophets, with Christ Jesus himself as the cornerstone. In him the whole structure is joined together and grows into a holy temple in the Lord" (Ephesians 2:20-21). In this text Paul used the Greek word *naos*, which translates into the "inner sanctuary," the holy of holies. This is the place where God comes to meet us. And God's presence, the Bible tells us, makes the church a holy place. Messy or not.

One spring day, I conducted a wedding for a couple. They had really been through a lot. She was twenty-eight and never married. He was thirty-two and had five children (ages thirteen, eleven, and nine-year-old triplets), all of whom lived with him. This was the third time their wedding had been scheduled. As I walked with them through the premarital classes, I came to appreciate their courage, honesty, sense of humor, and hopefulness. I've never seen a couple work so hard just to get married. Her mother didn't mind him or his kids so much, but she was worried about what a burden this huge, new family would be on her young daughter. His mother had been her grandchildren's surrogate mother for so long that she wasn't sure she could trust anyone else to do the job. And pretty much nobody was crazy about me. "Whaddya mean, a woman minister? Is that allowed?" I started off the rehearsal by reassuring everyone that, yes, this marriage would be legal. Then I smiled as big as I could at them and was happy to see a few cautious smiles back. Finally, when the day came, I arrived at the chapel and put on my vestments. Then I went out to meet the rest of the family and make sure everything was on schedule. I didn't get far before I saw the kids standing in the back of the church, looking very handsome—and very nervous—in their little tuxedos and matching dresses. I went over to introduce myself. "Hi," I said, "I'm Pastor Kelly."

They all told me their names and ages. Then one of the older boys asked, "Are you the priest?"

"I guess you could say that," I said.

"Are you the one who's going to help our dad get married?" asked one of the triplets.

"Yep, that would be me. That's just what I'm going to do." Then one of the girls took my hand and looked at me with such wise and serious eyes that, for a moment, everything stopped and became clearer than ever before. "You are beautiful," she said.

You are beautiful. Those words bounced around in my head for months, lifting my spirits and making me smile. Now, I'd like to think that she meant that I was beautiful. And maybe she did, a little. Children are not usually very discriminating. But you know what I think she really meant? I think she really meant that it was beautiful ... the fact that I was willing to help her dad get married. The fact that, because I was there, she knew somehow God was there and a part of what was happening too. Even the fact, I think, that I am a girl. Like her.

And you know what? She was right. That *is* beautiful. There really is nothing more beautiful than the church when we get it right. There is nothing more wonderful than the community of God's people gathered together to sing and to learn and to share and to grow. There is nothing more amazing than a community that has grace at its very heart where everyone is welcome and everyone is loved ... and everyone knows their job is to share that love with the world. There is nothing more holy. Messy or not.

By God's grace, the church has done some wonderful things over the centuries. Public education and public health care both began with the church. Churches have provided a starting point or foundation for the work of leaders like Martin Luther King Jr., Dorothy Day, and Mother Teresa. Churches have given sanctuary to people in all kinds of trouble in places around the world. Today, churches are first on the scene with relief aid wherever there is a natural disaster, a famine, a war. There is nothing more wonderful than when, in spite of ourselves, we get it right and let God work through the church.

A given

The community of God's people is a holy mess. But beyond that, for God's people, community is just a given. That's how it's been from the beginning. Jesus never had to tell his friends to "go to church." They *were* the church. And they wouldn't have known how to do it any other way.

When those earliest Christians answered Jesus' call to "Come, follow me," they joined Jesus' posse. For Peter and the other disciples, answering this call was never all about "me and Jesus." It can't be that way for you or me today either. To be a Christian is to participate in God's mission to bring the whole world back home again. That is something no one of us could ever possibly accomplish alone. We need each other.

Jesus' early followers were as devoted to each other as they were to God. They prayed together and "broke bread" together and took up a collection to help the poor. They weren't looking for perfection—they were looking for protection. They were looking for the kind of encouragement they could only get from others who were walking the same path, facing the same challenges, wrestling with the same doubts and demons. They never thought of trying to move forward on their own. They needed each other and they knew it. In each other they found their strength (read Acts 2:37-47).

Jesus knew we would need each other too. That's why one of the very last things he told his disciples was this: "This is my commandment, that you love one another as I have loved you" (John 15:12). Jesus warned his disciples that they would face hard times. Those who oppose me, Jesus told them, will make it difficult to keep your promises to me, to hold on to your faith, to do the things you know I want you to do. Hang on to each other for dear life, he said.

For God's people, the church is just a given. We need each other. And we're stuck with each other. So we might as well love each other, the way Jesus loves us. Love each other even when we're crabby. Love each other even when we're wrong. Love each other even through our differences and our disappointments. And when faced with those we consider the least lovable or deserving characters of all—welcome them and love them. Like that grown-up kid eating Thanksgiving turkey. The one who looks a little embarrassed as the story of the telltale trike is told again.

Love the ones who seem to least deserve it, most of all.

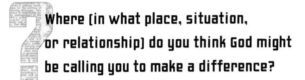

Where [in what place, situation, or relationship] do you think God might be calling you to make a difference?

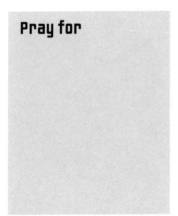

Pray for

"You shall love the Lord your God with all your heart, and with all your soul, and with all your mind." This is the greatest and first commandment. And a second is like it: "You shall love your neighbor as yourself."
Matthew 22:37-39

8 | WARNING: CROSSROADS

This business of Bible study is about transformation. Through the Bible, God speaks to us. Expect to be comforted. Expect to be challenged. Expect to be changed.

People do a lot of weird things with their lives. But Takeru Kobayashi takes the cake. Actually, Kobayashi prefers hot dogs. He is a professional "speed eater." And for four years in a row, he has won the world hot-dog eating contest, held every year on Coney Island on the Fourth of July. Begun in 1916, the contest is a very serious business. Twenty competitors from across the globe gather together to out eat each other. Japan's Kobayashi, a lean, mean, eating machine, has become a legend, setting a new world record. He not only defeats his opponents, he out wolfs them.

In 2000, Kazutoyo Arai broke the world record at Coney Island by eating 25 hot dogs in twelve minutes. The following year, Kobayashi showed up. A skinny teenager at the time, Kobayashi stunned the world of competitive eating by consuming a mind-boggling 50 hot dogs in twelve minutes. In 2004, he broke his own record by devouring 53 1/2 of them. His trademark is the "Solomon method," a hot-dog-eating technique he developed himself, in which he breaks the dog in two before swallowing each half whole. Observers report a kind of irresistible urge to keep watching, no matter how gross the whole thing becomes. Kobayashi just keeps eating. A member of the Competitive Eating Federation, he made $150,000 last year on the worldwide eating circuit. If you don't believe me, go online and do your own research.

You ain't heard nothing yet

But whatever you do, don't start shaking your head in disbelief. As weird as hot-dog-eating-your-way-through-life is, it is nothing compared to the kinds of things God asks people to do with their lives.

Think about it.

It is a beautifully cloudless day. And then the Lord shows up, umbrella in hand, and tells Noah to drop whatever he's doing and get cracking—he's got a boat to build. And when it was finished, the Lord spoke again. "Go into the ark," the Lord said, "you and all your household, for I have seen that you alone are righteous before me in this generation" (Genesis 7:1). Oh, and Noah, take as many animals as you can carry. His neighbors must have thought he was crazy. "Well," they probably said to each other in that knowing sort of way, "people do a lot of weird things with their lives."

And that's true. They do ... especially when they are following God.

Take Moses, for example. He was literally hiding out in Midian, far from the land of his birth, in a self-imposed exile after killing a guy there in a fit of rage. He knew if he stepped foot over the border, his life would be in danger. But then God showed up and basically said: Never mind all that, Moses. I need you to do something for me. You're going back to Egypt. You're going head to head with the Pharaoh. You're going to lead my people out of slavery and bring them back home again. "So Moses took his wife and his sons, put them on a donkey and went back to the land of Egypt; and Moses carried the staff of God in his hand" (Exodus 4:20).

This is crazy stuff.

No wonder, when God shows up on the scene as a principal figure, half the time people want to take off in the other direction.

Another prophet, Jonah, not only wanted to—he did. "Go!" the Lord had said to him: "Go at once to Nineveh, that great city and cry out against it; for their wickedness has come up before me" (Jonah 1:2). Yeah, right. Like he was going to walk right into the middle of *that* one. Eventually, Jonah did what God told him to do, but not until he was very nearly fish food.

Maybe it's because he had heard stories like that one that the prophet Isaiah didn't even blink when God showed up. When he heard the Lord asking, "Whom shall I send, and who will go for us?" Isaiah said, "Here am I; send me!" (Isaiah 6:8). He said that even though he knew it was going to get him into all kinds of hot water with priests and kings and everyone in between. One way or another, Isaiah had to have known there was no point arguing. If you're going to follow God, you've got to expect the unexpected.

Maybe the weirdest thing any of those biblical characters did comes right at the end of Jesus' story. He had his closest friends gathered around him. He was getting ready to say his farewell. Good Friday was still a fresh and painful memory, but Easter had dawned. It had also dawned on the disciples that something really important had happened there.

Jesus appeared to them one last time, and gave them this final instruction: "Go ... and make disciples of all nations, baptizing them in the name of the Father and the Son and the Holy Spirit, and teaching them to obey everything that I have commanded you. And remember, I am with you always, to the end of the age" (Matthew 28:19-20).

In Acts, they are promised the power of the Holy Spirit, and then they are left watching. Jesus disappears! He ascends into heaven. (Read Acts 1:6-11.) Is it any wonder the disciples just stood there scratching their heads? We're supposed to do WHAT? Where? WHO?!?! The ELEVEN of us?!?!

But they did it. Man oh man, did they do it. They are the reason you and I are here today.

With God in the lead, we can be sure some crazy stuff lies ahead. At least that's how I read the story. Throughout the Bible, God is always leading people into places they would never have gone on their own. God is always asking people to do things they would never have the courage to do by themselves. There is no taking the easy road. There is no standing still.

At the crossroads

It's no wonder that Jesus told people to "count the cost" before accepting his invitation to come and follow him. He warned the crowds who were tagging along behind him that following him, for real, would not be easy. But he didn't tell them that to scare them off. He just wanted them to know what they were getting themselves into. If you were going to build a tower, for example, or a house, wouldn't you sit down first and figure out what it was going to cost? Before you jump into following Jesus, don't you want to know what you're getting yourself into? (Read Luke 14:25-35.)

Jesus thought we should.

Jesus encourages us to be smart about our decision to follow him or not. We should know what we're getting into before we get on board. He won't try to fool us. Following Jesus is hard and often scary. Stepping out onto the path he has cut for us means leaving our own agendas there, at the crossroads.

I know a lot of people are in the habit of looking for wisdom in the Bible. It works like this: You have a problem or a question. And so you go to the Bible (one that has a fancy index in it) and you look for passages to assist you. You look for verses that talk about "sin," let's say, or "friendship" or "prayer" or "peace." And if your Bible has a subject guide, it identifies for you what verses to read. You read them, get what you need, and close the book confident that you've learned something important.

Maybe you have.

The Bible is, of course, a very wise book, but it is not to be used like an encyclopedia or a dictionary. Through the words in that book, a living God wants to speak a word to you. It may or may not be the word you were expecting or hoping for. But it will be God's word. And so it will be exactly what you need.

Following Jesus means being willing to set our agendas aside in order to listen for God's voice, calling us into new and unfamiliar territory. It means being willing to be led. It means being willing to be challenged and changed.

Expect to be challenged

I was pretty young when I first realized the way a relationship with someone can shape your identity. It was a lazy summer day. I was eleven years old. My friends and I went exploring. Well, okay, I went exploring. They dared me to. Dared me to step inside this old house that was rumored to be haunted. Or so we thought. For years it stood empty, deserted for as long as any of us could remember. Boarded windows and doors didn't seem to intimidate me. I went in. There weren't any ghosts around that I could see but it was an awfully stupid thing to do. The floorboards looked like they might give way under an intruding mouse, much less me. I scrambled out as soon as I could and still save face with my friends. Of course, it wasn't them I should have been worried about but my mom. My mom was furious. "But, Mom," I said, "all my friends were there too." That's when for the first time I can remember I heard these words: "I don't care what all your friends do. You are the one that I care about. You are my daughter."

And that, I realized, made me different.

As followers of Jesus, we *are* different. I'm not saying that we are perfect. We are as messed up, in every way, as anybody else is. We need to be saved; that's why God sent a Savior. No, we are not different because we are somehow more acceptable to God. We are different because God *expects* something of us. We are expected to listen to God, to take our cues from God's word, to seek out God's advice and direction. We are expected to live our lives as though being a child of God matters. We are expected to pour ourselves out for the sake of God's world, giving and witnessing and sharing. We are expected to serve. And this is not always an easy thing to do.

You know that big crowd that was following Jesus? Well, no wonder! Jesus invited everyone to follow him. But he never tried to hide the truth about what following him would mean. Not everyone was willing to make that kind of sacrifice. Even today it is hard. It means making a change in the way you live, in what is important to you. Listen to what he turned around and told that big crowd one day. He said something like this: You cannot be my disciple, unless you love me more than you love your father and mother, your wife and children, and your brothers and sisters. You cannot come with me unless you love me more than you love your own life. (Read Matthew 10:37-38 and Luke 14:26-27.) What he meant is that if you are going to be a follower of God, then nothing else can be more important to you than that. Yikes.

This would be no big deal, I suppose, to people who didn't have family or friends or safe places to sleep or cars that started even in the winter. But what about for those of us who do? Those of us who have been blessed with many things can get easily confused, forgetting which thing is the most important.

I really admire people who can keep it straight. A while back, in an interview, the successful actor Denzel Washington described writing a check for a million dollars, more or less on the spur of the moment, to Nelson Mandela's foundation to help the youth of South Africa. Washington explained his action by saying, "You never see a funeral hearse pulling a U-Haul behind it."

Being a follower of Jesus means, partly, being challenged to see past all the things in your life to the one thing that really matters.

That crowd following Jesus was probably as happy as could be. They were hearing great messages. Given his way with a few crumbs of food, they were never hungry. And I'm thinking nobody was ever sick for very long. But then there came that moment when Jesus turned to them and said: Choose. "Whoever does not carry the cross and follow me cannot be my disciple" (Luke 14:27). This moment of truth comes to everyone who wants to follow Jesus.

A friend of mine who has just recently turned the corner from being a spectator to being a participant on the journey of faith described the moment when he realized what had happened. "I realized that I could no longer make any decision just because it was good for *me!*" Now God is a part of his every move.

The fact is, every decision we are faced with becomes a crossroads of sorts. At every turn, we are faced with a choice. Some of those choices are small ones. Do I shake my fist and honk at that guy who cut me off during rush hour traffic or not? But sometimes the choices are huge. Do I quit this job because I am being asked to do things I know are hurtful to other people? Or do I stay because the money is so unbelievably good? Do I make a sacrificial gift to this organization I believe in? Or do I buy that new car? Answering the call to be a part of God's mission in the world means that, when you come to the crossroads, you go the way of Jesus. You go the way of truth and courage. You go the way of compassion and self-sacrifice. You do the right thing in everything. You lead with love.

Expect to be changed

I asked a class of sixty seminary students the other day if they could think of a single person in the Bible who had an encounter with God—and went away unchanged. They just looked at me with crooked smiles. "Judas?" one of them tried out.

"No!" said another. "Think about what happened to him. (Read Acts 1:12-26 for an obscure account of how Judas met his end.) It wasn't what you'd call a positive change. But it was definitely a change!"

They couldn't think of anyone.

Change is not only an inevitable part of life (if you're not changing, you're dead!), it's a certain outcome of an encounter with God. We are different people because God is in our lives.

Those sixteenth-century Lutheran reformers were so certain of this that they built it into the structure of their main document, the Augsburg Confession. Composed of a number of articles of faith, the document sums up their ideas about God and the church and the Christian life. The first few articles basically say that God created everything and we keep messing it up. Article 4 describes God's amazing gift of love and our salvation through Jesus Christ. Article 5 discusses the way in which this gift comes to us in the Word of God. And Article 6 (are you ready for this?!) tells us that the first fruit of salvation is a changed life. In other words, we expect something to happen in a life once Jesus is in it. There is a change. There is a conversion. There is transformation.

And if you don't believe them and you don't believe me, maybe you'll believe Aunt Minnie.

Aunt Minnie is one of my heroes. She was a member of the first congregation I served as pastor and she was, in fact, everybody's aunt. She had never married, and had lived alone and supported herself her whole long life. She was about ninety when we met. The congregation was full of her nieces and nephews, but we all called her Aunt Minnie. Even me.

Well, this was a wonderful congregation, out in the country. It was 125 years old and it was beautiful. It was one of those white clapboard buildings with a steeple and a bell that still got rung every Sunday by hand. I loved that place. But folks there would be the first to tell you that it was a pretty traditional place. When I arrived, there had never been a woman elected to serve on council. As pastor, I was the first one.

There I was—a young, energetic pastor right out of seminary, ready to take on the world—in a congregation where little new had happened in a very long time. I was full of ideas! "How can I shake things up a little?" I thought. "I need something really radical." And then it came to me. Talk to Aunt Minnie!

Off I went to the Lutheran Home where Aunt Minnie was living. Aunt Minnie still worshiped with us every Sunday, even after she moved out of her own home. She'd get in that big old Buick of hers and drive up and down those narrow dusty country roads without any regard for her safety, or ours! Yet somehow everybody knew—*wink, wink*—what roads she took, and I guess they just stayed clear of them.

I told Aunt Minnie what was on my mind. "Aunt Minnie," I said, "what do you think about the idea of having members of the congregation read Scripture during worship on Sunday mornings?" (Told you it was radical.)

Actually, it was.

Up until that point, the pastor led worship and no one assisted (well, unless you count the organist, who was seated at her bench, thank you very much). And I got it in my head that asking lay people to be lectionary readers would be just the eye-popping new thing we needed to get the blood flowing in that congregation.

Aunt Minnie just looked at me. I can only imagine what she was thinking of this crazy young pastor and her crazy idea and the crazy way she kept insisting that God was up to something. And I think, finally, THAT was the thing that got her attention. God WAS up to something. And Aunt Minnie knew it.

Now, you need to know something about Aunt Minnie in order for this story to make sense. Aunt Minnie had been active in Bible study for decades—long before I was even born. Month in and month out, Aunt Minnie and her women friends would gather together to read God's Word and learn to identify the sound of God's voice.

And that day, when she heard God's voice, she didn't hesitate. She got a gleam in her eye like I had never seen before. She told me that not only did she find the idea inspired she'd help where she could. However, I had to promise her that we'd go about introducing this change HER way.

I'm no dummy. I agreed.

Aunt Minnie's plan started with this directive: Tell no one. She would be the first lay reader in that congregation and she knew just how to make it happen.

When the day came, Aunt Minnie drove out to worship just like always. Parked her Buick just like always. Got out her walker and ambled on into that old country church just like always. But that's where the pattern stopped. That day she didn't sit in her usual spot. No. Instead she sat at the back of the sanctuary as far away from ME as you could get.

At 10 o'clock the service started. I led as usual and gave no hint of the impending change. And when it came time for the readings I did as I had been instructed: I simply sat down. Now, you can imagine how hard it was for me to stay seated when people began to whisper. I could hear those closest to the front start to wonder aloud: "Did she forget?" "What's wrong with her?!?" "Is she sick?"

In the interim, Aunt Minnie, assisted by her walker, began to make her move. She stood up, and once steadied, made her way to the lectern—as slow as one could imagine. All eyes were on her. Her eyes were on me. But no one said a word. After all, this was Aunt Minnie.

At the lectern she appeared strong. She opened the Bible and began to read—like she had done this a million times before.

When she had finished, she took hold of her walker and set out to return to her seat—again as slow as humanly possible. Speed was not her intent.

And the whispers, they stopped. In fact, no one said anything that day. But from then on lay readers assisted—every Sunday morning—but they sat up front.

It is no coincidence that it was Aunt Minnie who led that congregation into a new day. This was a woman whose life had been shaped by the Word of God, and by the biblical stories. This was someone who had practice listening for God's voice. And when she heard it, she HEARD it!

Something happened that Sunday morning! It was as if somebody had opened all the windows and doors, and fresh air blew through. Some of us believed it was the Holy Spirit. Suddenly, all kinds of new things were possible! There was a new energy and a new vision. People joined the congregation! Bible studies started up. Dozens of folks showed up at adult forums. A budget was written and passed for the first time in the congregation's history, giving us the opportunity to think about what God was calling us to do—and be intentional about making it happen. Worship attendance grew by fifty percent in just a few short years, even though our church sat in the middle of a county that lost more people in a given year than almost any other county in the state. And our denomination chose that congregation to be the site of a regional rural ministry conference. People started dreaming again about what could be. That congregation was never exactly the same after that.

Neither was I. And neither was Aunt Minnie.

Somebody probably ought to warn you now that reading your Bible is a dangerous exercise. You won't be the same person when you're done.

Never alone

Those of us who have heard God's call to follow—and answered it—can expect to never stand still. "Go!" God calls to us, again and again.

Notice, though, that when Jesus called his friends to "Go!" there was no way he was going to send them out on that crazy mission of his without making sure they first had a promise to hang on to. He promised that they would never be alone.

It's amazing what you're able to do when you know somebody has your back covered. I mean, really, do you think there has ever been a solitary hero? There is always somebody behind the scenes, urging and encouraging, chasing that person down to tell her or him to get back to work and holding that person up when she or he may have fallen down. History is too often told as the story of *the heroic person*. Martin Luther King Jr.! Abraham Lincoln! Sojourner Truth! Sally Ride! This is crazy. There are always heroic *teams*.

One historian has argued that the real secret behind the American Revolution wasn't the grand ideas about democracy or the brilliant crafting of legal documents or the creation of inspired institutions. No. The real secret was the fact that the main characters in this whole drama—George Washington, Alexander Hamilton, Thomas Jefferson, James Madison, and Benjamin Franklin—were friends. They ate and drank together. They stayed up late into the night arguing with each other. They yelled and swore at each other. They knew that what they were doing was dangerous—and that one day they might even die together. They knew they were changing the world.

Rosa Parks didn't take her seat in the front of that bus all alone. And Martin Luther King Jr. wasn't the only one to have a dream. These amazing people had a whole community of people praying for them, willing to go to jail with them, and cheering them on. NASA always shoots at least three brave souls into space at a time; and behind them a whole command post is hard at work in Houston. The suffragettes linked arms and hiked up those overflowing skirts and marched together.

Jesus doesn't send his followers out alone on God's mission. We are sent out together. And Jesus promises to be right there with us, even *in* us, all along. He's got our back.

Imagine

Imagine following God into new places. Imagine doing things so scary and so hard that you would never even think to do them if left on your own. Even with Jesus at your back, you have to admit, *this* is a weird way to live.

And I can't imagine it any other way.

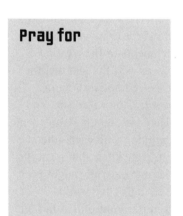

Where (in what place, situation, or relationship) do you think God might be calling you to make a difference?

Pray for

Whoever does not carry the cross and follow me cannot be my disciple.

Luke 14:27

For Reflection and Discussion

T hink about these questions on your own. Then consider using them to talk about the book with a *No Experience Necessary* small group or at least one or two other people. In your discussions, you can learn from each other and encourage each other to get to work in God's mission.

Chapter 1: Strange, But Wonderful

1. God actively tries to communicate with us through the Bible. How do you feel about this?

2. How did you picture God when you were growing up? How do you picture God now?

3. What do you find strange about who God is and what God is up to? What do you find wonderful about who God is and what God is up to?

Chapter 2: The Adventure of a Lifetime

1. You have a job to do in God's mission to save and bless the world. What's your reaction to this?

2. In your own words, what gives your life meaning?

3. Tell about one way that God has been using you to change the world.

Chapter 3: A Lifetime of Adventure

1. The characters we read about in the Bible weren't any better people than the rest of us. What do you think about this?

2. Tell about a time when God used you as a priest or bridge builder to reach someone.

3. What blessing from God can you use to bless others?

Chapter 4: No Experience Necessary

1. What words would you use to describe the Bible? Try to do this in just three words, if you can.

2. How can you make reading the Bible a regular part of your life?

3. What person or group can you meet with to study the Bible?

Chapter 5: Expect Great Things

1. In your prayer life, do you speak more or listen more? Would you like to change anything about this?
   (If your answer is "yes," what would you change?)

2. When do you find it easy to pray? When do you find it difficult to pray?

3. What do you do when it's difficult for you to pray?

Chapter 6: The Liver Incident

1. What do you see when you "walk the land"? What blessings has God given to you? Name as many as you can.

2. It might be corny, but try this little exercise anyway. If you were stranded on a desert island with no hope of rescue, what five material things (excluding people and pets) would you most like to have with you?

3. List some ways you can share or give away your stuff and yourself.

Chapter 7: The Telltale Trike

1. How does your community or congregation usually deal with conflict?

2. If a friend or neighbor asked you why you bother to spend any time at all with Christians or in a congregation, what would you say?

3. What difference would it make if more of us would *be* the church instead of *going to* church?

Chapter 8: Warning: Crossroads

1. Do you know someone like Aunt Minnie—someone who has learned to listen for God's voice through reading and studying the Bible? If you do, share a story about that person.

2. As you are sent out on God's mission, who are the people encouraging you, supporting you, and praying for you?

3. Where (in what place, situation, or relationship) do you think God might be calling you to make a difference?

For Further Reading and Study

- For a solid series of commentaries providing an in-depth look at each book in the Bible in pretty accessible language, use the Interpretation Commentary Series (Westminster/John Knox).

- To learn more about the mission of God, and our mission as Christians and members of the church, pick up *A Story Worth Sharing: Engaging Evangelism*, edited by Kelly A. Fryer (Augsburg Fortress, 2004). This book offers practical suggestions for carrying out God's mission in our lives and in our congregations.

- To listen for God's voice in the Bible, see the No Experience Necessary Bible study series written by Kelly A. Fryer (Augsburg Fortress, 2005). This series for small groups was inspired by the original 1999 edition of the book *No Experience Necessary.*

- For answers to basic questions like, "Who is Jesus?" and "Why bother about sin?"—questions you might be asking yourself as you read the Bible—look for *Christian Faith: The Basics* by Walt Kallestad (Augsburg Fortress, 1999).

- For help getting acquainted (or reacquainted) with words that are part of the Christian vocabulary, read *Amazing Grace: A Vocabulary of Faith* by Kathleen Norris (Riverhead Books, 1999).

- To experience the biblical story in a totally new way, read *The Book of God* by Walter Wangerin Jr. (Zondervan, 1996). This is a novel featuring the Bible's most dramatic characters.